FENG SHUI
for
HOMEBUYERS
INTERIOR

Feng Shui for Homebuyers - Interior

The author can be reached at:

Mastery Academy of Chinese Metaphysics Sdn. Bhd. (611143-A)
19-3, The Boulevard, Mid Valley City,
59200 Kuala Lumpur, Malaysia.

Tel   : +603-2284 8080
Fax   : +603-2284 1218
Email   : info@masteryacademy.com
Website : www.masteryacademy.com

DISCLAIMER:

Published by JY Books Sdn. Bhd. (659134-T)

INDEX

Preface

A classic mistake that many people make today when it comes to evaluating the Feng Shui of a property is to only look inside the house. Feng Shui today is done almost inside out. Instead of ensuring the house conforms with the external macro environment, they seek to make the environment conform to the house. This is a wrong approach.

Hence, this book has been written primarily as a companion to my other book, *Feng Shui for Homebuyers – Exterior*. The interior Feng Shui of a house should only be considered after the environmental features, such as the mountains and rivers, surrounding the property are evaluated. The quality of Feng Shui on a property is almost completely dependent on the quality of the external environment and the Qi that the property receives. Interior Feng Shui is mainly used to dictate how the Qi enters the property and how it is circulated and utilised in the home.

This book allows you to recognise, by observing appearances or forms, what is good and what is not good when it comes to the interior of a house. From the moment you step into a house, have this book with you. It will provide you with a checklist of dos and don'ts that should enable you to decide whether or not to buy the house, based on the interior.

However, if you have already purchased a property, do not be disheartened. This book will be able to help you ensure that you get the interior Feng Shui right – this way, you may not have fantastic Feng Shui but at the very least, you will not have unfavourable Feng Shui inside your home.

Much of the inspiration for this book came from architects, interior designers and real estate agents who want a way to better understand Feng Shui without having to learn formulas or take a class.

The truth is, when it comes to interior Feng Shui, not having any formulas is quite difficult. Formulas are needed to verify the Qi in the house, both externally and internally. But I also realise that aside from architects, interior designers and real estate agents, formulas are also not favoured by the lay public. The lay public want something that is easy to use, which doesn't require a lot of brain cracking and calculation and too much basic knowledge.

This was certainly a real challenge but I believe that I have managed to keep this book as fuss-free and formula-free as I can. There is a little bit of formula used but I have tried to ensure that it is of the 'maximum benefit, minimum effort' kind! I will introduce generic formulas that safetly to a majority of houses.

Ultimately of course, calculations and formula applications are the purview of the professional Classical Feng Shui consultant, especially since there are literally hundreds of formulas in the ancient classics, most which require some form of formal study to understand and apply. So remember that this book is designed to enable you to do some Do-It-Yourself (DIY) Feng Shui and screen properties, but it is not a substitute for a proper consultation from a qualified Classical Feng Shui consultant.

But at the same time, I believe that most people don't mind doing a little work and making some effort to screen properties. Certainly, there are a lot of benefits to doing a little legwork yourself. First, you save consulting fees because rather than getting the consultant to check all the houses on your list, you just get the consultant to check the final 2-3 choices. Secondly, the consultant can focus on improving the house to make the Feng Shui better, rather than telling you how to fix it just to make it 'not bad' Feng Shui. Frankly, as a Feng Shui Consultant, I don't like to give people bad news. I'd much rather tell my clients how to spend money improving their Feng Shui, than tell them how to spend money fixing the flaws and then spending more to improve the Feng Shui.

Through this book, I also hope to make everyone's life a little easier – the client, the interior designer, the contractor, the architect and that of the Feng Shui consultant! When the client starts out with a good house and good basic interior Feng Shui, unnecessary cost, inconvenience and problems are greatly reduced.

I've also written this book with a view to providing some guidance and information for interior designers and architects, who often find themselves having to change their designs to accommodate Feng Shui concerns. By understanding how Feng Shui works inside a property, interior designers will be able to avoid designs or renovations that may create Feng Shui problems and at the same time, create designs or undertake improvements that rectify or fix flaws. For architects, this book will help you ensure you do not create inadvertently, negative Feng Shui in a property. If the blueprints of a house avoid key Feng Shui flaws, then the Feng Shui consultant's job is made easier and there will be fewer debates too between the parties!

Real estate agents will also find this book helpful, I believe, as it will enable them to provide some simple advice or guidance to clients on how to fix or rectify certain flaws inside the house, before putting it on the market for sale or rental. This way, you and your client dodge the 'Bad Feng Shui' bullet and at the same time, increase or enhance the attractiveness of your property by ensuring that it has minimum Feng Shui flaws.

For homebuyers out there, I hope you enjoy reading this book and I wish you all the best in finding the house of your dreams, complete with positive Feng Shui Quotient!

Warmest Regards,

Joey Yap

February 2006

Author's personal website: www.joeyyap.com
Academy website: www.masteryacademy.com | www.masteryjournal.com

MASTERY ACADEMY
OF CHINESE METAPHYSICS™

At www.masteryacademy.com, you will find some useful tools to ascertain key information about the Feng Shui of a property or for study of Astrology.

To learn more about your personal Destiny, you can use the Joey Yap BaZi Ming Pan Calculator to plot your Four Pillars of Destiny – you just need to have your date of birth (day, month, year) and time of birth. The Joey Yap Flying Star Calculator can be utilised to plot your home or office Flying Star chart. To find out your personal best directions, use the 8 Mansions Calculator.

For more information about BaZi, Xuan Kong or Flying Star Feng Shui, or if you wish to learn more about these subjects with Joey Yap, logon to the Mastery Academy of Chinese Metaphysics website at **www.masteryacademy.com.**

Chapter One: Introduction to using Feng Shui

Feng Shui is very much a word the public knows these days. There are very few people who haven't heard about it. Unfortunately, in the process of taking Feng Shui to the public domain, it has very much become a simplified practice. Everything is boiled down to 'good' or 'bad', 'auspicious' and 'inauspicious'. Sometimes, logic and rationale are lost in the rush to take Feng Shui to the widest possible market. Hence, while it seems strange, I believe it is important that you understand how to use Feng Shui, before you start to use it!

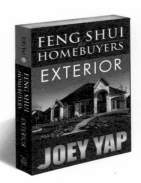

My previous book, **Feng Shui for Homebuyers – Exterior**, delves into what Feng Shui is all about and how it is a goal-driven practice. My other book, *Stories and Lessons on Feng Shui*, delves into why Feng Shui is not just about making money or enhancing 'good luck'.

What I want to touch on here, in this introductory chapter, is how we should regard Feng Shui. From the most sophisticated formulas, to the simplest Feng Shui systems, it is always important to understand that Feng Shui is more than just 'good' and 'bad'. We want to ask: what exactly is bad, how bad it is, and why it is bad in the first place.

For example, most people know that they shouldn't sleep under a beam. This is one of those Feng Shui principles that has become part of the public knowledge and consciousness. But most of the time, people have no idea why they shouldn't be sleeping under a beam. They just know they shouldn't. It is precisely this sort of thinking that needs to be avoided in Feng Shui and it is this kind of thinking that leads to superstition and needless paranoia.

*Beams suppress Qi but it is also important to ask,
what is being suppressed?*

Beams are considered a negative environmental form because it suppresses Qi. Frequently, there is also no real understanding of what is actually affected by the beam in the bedroom. For example, what is the difference between a beam in the Yan Nian (延年) sector of a room, and the Wu Gui (五鬼) sector of a room? If a consultant understands what type of Qi is affected by the beam, he or she can determine where and what exactly the problem is. If Yan Nian is suppressed, relationships become a problem. If Wu Gui is suppressed, then backstabbing problems are likely.

Knowing something to be simply 'good' or 'bad' creates a lot of misunderstanding, paranoia and fear. It is important to understand that Feng Shui is not blanket superstition. In Feng Shui, everything has a reason, a justification. Of course, because this is meant to be a simple book, there are few technicalities and a lot of the information has been boiled down to make it easy and simple to understand. But that does not mean that what you are learning here is without rationale or has no grounding in the classics.

風水

Basic Feng Shui 101

There are several key concepts that must be understood before you can use Feng Shui. They are the concept of Qi, stars and Forms. You need to understand these simple basics and appreciate how they are inter-related in the study of Feng Shui.

What is Qi? This may sound like a silly question but often, people don't really understand what Qi is. Qi essentially is a body of energy that circulates and permeates the world we live in. Qi is the life force or the invisible force that shapes, nurtures and governs all living beings. From the peak of the highest mountains to the depth of the deepest oceans, the flow of the rivers to the undulating ridges of the land, and from busy malls to the quaint little corners of the street - Qi permeates our world. Qi is the force that brings life to all beings.

It is a naturally occurring phenomenon in nature and the environment and cannot be made or manufactured artificially. So no, your haircut, t-shirt colour and a dragon figurine made of resin do not emanate Qi nor do they influence the Qi in your environment or your home.

Qi is the core and backbone of Feng Shui. The basic objective of interior Feng Shui is to draw in and circulate positive Qi within the house so that the positive Qi in the house can benefit and support the endeavours of the residents.

The purpose of formulas and systems like Eight Mansions (八宅), Flying Stars (飛星), Xuan Kong Da Gua 64 (玄空大卦), San He (三合), and San Yuan (三元), is to obtain a Qi map of a property or an area and determine what energies reside in which sector by looking at what stars are located in which sector.

Hence, when you see the word 'stars' in Feng Shui, it is not a reference to the stars in the sky or astrological phenomenon. Rather, stars in the context of Feng Shui, and in the classical texts, is simply an abbreviation or code for types of Qi. Usually, stars go by numerical references (such as in Flying Stars) or by names (such as Greedy Wolf Tang Lang (貪狼), or Military Arts Wu Qu (武曲)). Stars also have elemental values based on the Five Elements (Water, Fire, Wood, Earth, Metal) assigned to them.

Forms or Luan Tou (巒頭) which translates loosely into 'Faces of the Mountain' essentially refers to the environmental features in the macro environment of a property such as mountains and rivers or water. It is the big picture. This big picture matters because without the macro, there can be no micro. *Feng Shui for Homebuyers - Exterior* goes into quite a bit of detail on external environmental features and forms and explains how to read forms, even in this modern day of skyscrapers and highways. Forms, on a smaller scale can refer to the interior set up of a property. The way the rooms are laid out, the shape, size and space are referred to as 'Interior Forms'.

The Qi on a property is governed by the stars and the Forms. By understanding what stars reside in which sectors of the property, we are able to then decide how best to utilise that area or at least understand what potential (or setbacks) it presents, based on the nature of the energies in each sector. Stars are mapped out by calculations, based on the direction of your property while Forms, which are the physical external and internal environmental features, are determined by observation.

In recent years, there has been some confusion in the public between what has become known as the Compass School and the Forms School. This is an unfortunate misconception that has occurred due to some of the translation work done on ancient Feng Shui texts.

There is no such thing as a "Compass" school of Feng Shui in Classical Feng Shui. For that matter, all systems of Feng Shui, whether they are based on Qi or Forms, make use of a compass. If you encounter a Feng Shui consultant who does not use a compass, then you should be very concerned.

Where there is a difference of opinion is between what is known as the Li Qi (理氣) or Theory of Qi School of Feng Shui and the Luan Tou (巒頭) or Forms (形法) School of Feng Shui. However, neither of these schools advocates a 'all or nothing' approach. In other words, both schools recognise that Qi and Forms go together, but simply differ on the priority they accord to Qi and Forms.

So, the Li Qi School bases most of the assessment of a property on formulas and sophisticated calculations to ascertain the Qi map of the property. The focus of the Li Qi school is to ascertain the energy map of the property. The calculation can be done largely on paper. By contrast, the Luan Tou or Forms school, focuses on formulas as well, but form-based formulas. The Forms school is based on physical observation of the environment – so the consultant has to be at the site to observe the forms in the area. Forms today extend to include man-made architectural features that are often found in modern city and urban living. At the advanced level, Forms enable the understanding of what kind of natural Qi is produced by the environment and what kind of man-made structure or architectural features are best able to contain the Qi found in the environment.

How Stars, Qi and Forms Inter-relate

In Feng Shui, there is an ancient saying: "Forms activate stars, stars in turn affect the residents". Forms determine how the Qi, which are determined by the stars, react at any given time. Forms, interior or exterior, facilitate the flow of Qi via the stars. Good forms can enhance the quality of a positive star and smooth out the negative energies while bad forms, conversely, can aggravate negative stars and nullify the good energies.

Negative Qi needs negative forms before it can release any malevolent impact. Benevolent Qi requires positive forms in order to be beneficial. This Qi in turn, affects either positively or negatively, the residents who live in the property. Accordingly, Forms MUST interact with the Stars to create a positive or negative outcome in any given scenario. This is how Feng Shui works.

A simple way of understanding how forms, the property and the interior of the property interact is to think of an electric circuit. Imagine external forms as the energy source. The building (such as a house) is the conductor of the energy source. The interior forms of the house are the switch that determines if you can make use of the energy from the source. Without the appropriate forms, the building has no source of energy. And you can't turn something on if there's no power source. Similarly, you can't make use of a power supply, if there's no switch.

For this reason, it is not good enough to just apply Feng Shui formulas to a property without looking at the forms.

Many practitioners of Feng Shui tend to work from the inside out. They spend all their effort, energy and money fixing the interior of a home or trying to enhance the stars or Qi in an area, without really realising that what is outside their front door matters much more than what is inside. You cannot make the natural environment conform to the house, you must make the house conform to the environment. This is the basic underlying concept of Feng Shui – to fine-tune your property to benefit from the existing Qi of the immediate environment.

Similarly, having a good environment with benevolent Qi is completely wasted if the building that sits on the property does not receive or collect Qi through its Main Door, and if the interior forms within the building, such as the corridors, staircase and important rooms, do not circulate Qi or collect Qi. You see, forms are not just limited to the external environment – you also have internal forms, which is what this book is all about.

There are lots of advantages to applying Forms-based Feng Shui. Firstly, it is perception and observation based – most people have no difficulty determining if something is sharp or pointy, and also, making out shapes. Secondly, it is relatively simple to apply – there are no complicated calculations or specialised equipment needed.

Formulas and Forms

Whilst *Feng Shui for Homebuyers – Exterior* was completely formula-free, there is a small amount of formula in this book. But do not be alarmed – a majority of the techniques and methods used in this book are still observation-based and derived from Forms study.

Also, remember that if you can't figure out how to apply the formula, it is perfectly fine. I always tell my students, never let what you can't do get in the way of what you can do. Focus on observing the forms then and leave the formula to the consultant. In any case, if you get the forms right, then the Feng Shui of the property's interior, whilst it won't be ideal, will at least be pretty good.

The formula-based system that I will be mainly referring to in this book is known as the Eight Mansions system, or Ba Zhai. Eight Mansions is mainly an interior Feng Shui system and is primarily used by Feng Shui masters to understand the basic energy map of the property and enable proper use of the internal sectors of the house. It is a long-term system, designed for long-term results, rather than short-term results. It is a system that works more steadily, therefore it is an extremely suitable system to be used for homebuyers because people often buy a house for life, or at least, to occupy for a good number of years. This does not mean Eight Mansions is a superior system to any other system – each system has its advantages and disadvantages.

Ba
Zhai

I will only be using a very small percentage of the scope of Eight Mansions Feng Shui. My forthcoming book on Eight Mansions Feng Shui will delve into Eight Mansions more extensively. Also, this is not by any means the only system for evaluating interior Feng Shui. But it is a relatively easy system to explain and use by most people, which is also why I have chosen this system for this book.

An Introduction to
Eight Mansions System 八宅風水

Eight Mansions is one of the few classical Feng Shui systems widely practiced by Feng Shui Masters today. It belongs to the San Yuan School of Feng Shui and it has its basis in the quality of Qi as governed by the Trigram (卦) of the property and matching the property's energy (House Gua 宅卦) to the individual energies (Life Gua 命卦).

Trigrams are essentially a pictogram of lines used to depict the Yin and Yang occurrence of Qi. There are eight basic Trigrams, and they form what is known as the Ba Gua. Each of these trigrams represents a unique pattern of Qi. Basic Feng Shui begins with understanding how these eight basic Trigrams take form in a home, so that we can understand the Qi flow in a property.

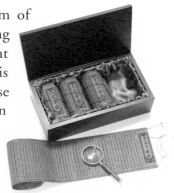

In Eight Mansions Feng Shui, a house has a governing trigram known as the House Gua. An individual, by virtue of his or her birthdate, also has a governing personal trigram known as the Life Gua. The basic idea of Eight Mansions Feng Shui is quite simple – match the house to the individual. To do this, we must first understand the connection between the House Gua and the Life Gua.

The Eight Mansions system harks back to the Yellow Emperor House Mansions Classics. However, back then, the system only utilised the House Gua method. Subsequent classics from the Qing Dynasty such as Eight Mansions Guiding Mirror (八宅明鏡) and Golden Star Classics (金光斗臨經) outline the importance of using the House Gua along with the Life Gua, along with special techniques called Inter-relationship between the Stars and Palaces Method (星宫生剋) which deals with understanding each of the elements of the eight stars in Eight Mansions Feng Shui.

The reason it is called Eight Mansions is because there are eight types of House Guas and essentially the system operates on the idea that there are eight types of houses, to be used by eight types of people. Practitioners of Eight Mansions usually need to be able to marry the House Gua and the Life Gua, through a technique known as matching people to the house. The skill of an Eight Mansions Feng Shui practitioner lies in being able to open up the house in a way that enables all the occupants to benefit from the property.

13

The Life Gua and House Gua in Eight Mansions

In Eight Mansions Feng Shui (八宅風水), there are two extremely important concepts that form the backbone of Eight Mansions: the Life Gua (命卦) and the House Gua (宅卦).

The Life Gua system or Ming Gua system is where the Favourable Directions or personal directions for the individual are derived. These personal directions are based on the 8 Cardinal directions: North, Northwest, Northeast, South, Southwest, Southeast, East, and West. There are four favourable or auspicious directions (Sheng Qi 生氣, Tian Yi 天醫, Yan Nian 延年 and Fu Wei 伏位) and four unfavourable or inauspicious directions (Huo Hai 禍害, Liu Sha 六煞, Jue Ming 絕命 and Wu Gui 五鬼). Which directions are favourable and unfavourable vary according to the person's Gua.

There are eight basic Gua groups represented by a number of the Gua. Determining the Life Gua involves a simple formula calculation based on a person's year of birth. However, to make it easy for you, I have included an extensive Gua table in the pages overleaf. So just find your year of birth and your Gua number is in the corresponding column.

Once you have determined your Gua, you can then ascertain your personal auspicious and inauspicious directions. All Guas are either part of the East Group of directions, or the West Group of directions. For ease of reference, I have reproduced overleaf, a table with the auspicious and inauspicious directions for all the eight Guas.

Eight Mansions Life Gua Reference Table

生肖 Animal	出生年 Year of Birth		Gua Number for 命卦		出生年 Year of Birth		Gua Number for 命卦	
			Male 男	Female 女			Male 男	Female 女
子 Rat	1912 壬子	Water Rat Ren Zi	7	8	1936 丙子	Fire Rat Bing Zi	1	8
丑 Ox	1913 癸丑	Water Ox Gui Chou	6	9	1937 丁丑	Fire Ox Ding Chou	9	6
寅 Tiger	1914 甲寅	Wood Tiger Jia Yin	2	1	1938 戊寅	Earth Tiger Wu Yin	8	7
卯 Rabbit	1915 乙卯	Wood Rabbit Yi Mao	4	2	1939 己卯	Earth Rabbit Ji Mao	7	8
辰 Dragon	1916 丙辰	Fire Dragon Bing Chen	3	3	1940 庚辰	Metal Dragon Geng Chen	6	9
巳 Snake	1917 丁巳	Fire Snake Ding Si	2	4	1941 辛巳	Metal Snake Xin Si	2	1
午 Horse	1918 戊午	Earth Horse Wu Wu	1	8	1942 壬午	Water Horse ren Wu	4	2
未 Sheep	1919 己未	Earth Goat Ji Wei	9	6	1943 癸未	Water Goat Gui Wei	3	3
申 Monkey	1920 庚申	Metal Monkey Geng Shen	8	7	1944 甲申	Wood Monkey Jia Shen	2	4
酉 Rooster	1921 辛酉	Metal Rooster Xin You	7	8	1945 乙酉	Wood Rooster Yi You	1	8
戌 Dog	1922 壬戌	Water Dog Ren Xu	6	9	1946 丙戌	Fire Dog Bing Xu	9	6
亥 Pig	1923 癸亥	Water Pig Gui Hai	2	1	1947 丁亥	Fire Pig Ding Hai	8	7
子 Rat	1924 甲子	Wood Rat Jia Zi	4	2	1948 戊子	Earth Rat Wu Zi	7	8
丑 Ox	1925 乙丑	Wood Ox Yi Chou	3	3	1949 己丑	Earth Ox Si Chou	6	9
寅 Tiger	1926 丙寅	Fire Tiger Bing Yin	2	4	1950 庚寅	Metal Tiger Geng Yin	2	1
卯 Rabbit	1927 丁卯	Fire Rabbit Ding Mao	1	8	1951 辛卯	Metal Rabbit Xin Mao	4	2
辰 Dragon	1928 戊辰	Earth Dragon Wu Chen	9	6	1952 壬辰	Water Dragon Ren Chen	3	3
巳 Snake	1929 己巳	Earth Snake Ji Si	8	7	1953 癸巳	Water Snake Gui Si	2	4
午 Horse	1930 庚午	Metal Horse Geng Wu	7	8	1954 甲午	Wood Horse Jia Wu	1	8
未 Sheep	1931 辛未	Metal Goat Xin Wei	6	9	1955 乙未	Wood Goat Yi Wei	9	6
申 Monkey	1932 壬申	Water Monkey Ren Shen	2	1	1956 丙申	Fire Monkey Bing Shen	8	7
酉 Rooster	1933 癸酉	Water Rooster Gui You	4	2	1957 丁酉	Fire Rooster Ding You	7	8
戌 Dog	1934 甲戌	Wood Dog Jia Xu	3	3	1958 戊戌	Earth Dog Wu Xu	6	9
亥 Pig	1935 乙亥	Wood Pig Yi Hai	2	4	1959 己亥	Earth Pig Ji Hai	2	1

Eight Mansions Life Gua Reference Table

生肖 Animal	出生年 Year of Birth		Gua Number for 命卦		出生年 Year of Birth		Gua Number for 命卦	
			Male 男	Female 女			Male 男	Female 女
子 Rat	1960 庚子	Metal Rat Geng Zi	4	2	1984 甲子	Wood Rat Jia Zi	7	8
丑 Ox	1961 辛丑	Metal Ox Xin Chou	3	3	1985 乙丑	Wood Ox Yi Chou	6	9
寅 Tiger	1962 壬寅	Water Tiger Ren Yin	2	4	1986 丙寅	Fire Tiger Bing Yin	2	1
卯 Rabbit	1963 癸卯	Water Rabbit Gui Mao	1	8	1987 丁卯	Fire Rabbit Ding Mao	4	2
辰 Dragon	1964 甲辰	Wood Dragon Jia Chen	9	6	1988 戊辰	Earth Dragon Wu Chen	3	3
巳 Snake	1965 乙巳	Wood Snake Yi Si	8	7	1989 己巳	Earth Snake Ji Si	2	4
午 Horse	1966 丙午	Fire Horse Bing Wu	7	8	1990 庚午	Metal Horse Geng Wu	1	8
未 Sheep	1967 丁未	Fire Goat Ding Wei	6	9	1991 辛未	Metal Goat Xin Wei	9	6
申 Monkey	1968 戊申	Earth Monkey Wu Shen	2	1	1992 壬申	Water Monkey Ren Shen	8	7
酉 Rooster	1969 己酉	Earth Rooster Ji You	4	2	1993 癸酉	Water Rooster Gui You	7	8
戌 Dog	1970 庚戌	Metal Dog Geng Xu	3	3	1994 甲戌	Wood Dog Jia Xu	6	9
亥 Pig	1971 辛亥	Metal Pig Xin Hai	2	4	1995 乙亥	Wood Pig Yi Hai	2	1
子 Rat	1972 壬子	Water Rat Ren Zi	1	8	1996 丙子	Fire Rat Bing Zi	4	2
丑 Ox	1973 癸丑	Water Ox Gui Chou	9	6	1997 丁丑	Fire Ox Ding Chou	3	3
寅 Tiger	1974 甲寅	Wood Tiger Jia Yin	8	7	1998 戊寅	Earth Tiger Wu Yin	2	4
卯 Rabbit	1975 乙卯	Wood Rabbit Yi Mao	7	8	1999 己卯	Earth Rabbit Ji Mao	1	8
辰 Dragon	1976 丙辰	Fire Dragon Bing Chen	6	9	2000 庚辰	Metal Dragon Geng Chen	9	6
巳 Snake	1977 丁巳	Fire Snake Ding Si	2	1	2001 辛巳	Metal Snake Xin Si	8	7
午 Horse	1978 戊午	Earth Horse Wu Wu	4	2	2002 壬午	Water Horse Ren Wu	7	8
未 Sheep	1979 己未	Earth Goat Ji Wei	3	3	2003 癸未	Water Goat Gui Wei	6	9
申 Monkey	1980 庚申	Metal Monkey Geng Shen	2	4	2004 甲申	Wood Monkey Jia Shen	2	1
酉 Rooster	1981 辛酉	Metal Rooster Xin You	1	8	2005 乙酉	Wood Rooster Yi You	4	2
戌 Dog	1982 壬戌	Water Dog Ren Xu	9	6	2006 丙戌	Fire Dog Bing Xu	3	3
亥 Pig	1983 癸亥	Water Pig Gui Hai	8	7	2007 丁亥	Fire Pig Ding Hai	2	4

• Please note that the date for the Chinese Solar Year starts on Feb 4.

This means that if you were born in Feb 2 of 2002, you belong to the previous year 2001.

East Group 東宅 Reference Table

Gua 卦	Sheng Qi 生氣	Tian Yi 天醫	Yan Nian 延年	Fu Wei 伏位	Huo Hai 禍害	Wu Gui 五鬼	Liu Sha 六煞	Jue Ming 絕命
Kan 坎 1 Water	South East 東南	East 東	South 南	North 北	West 西	North East 東北	North West 西北	South West 西南
Zhen 震 3 Wood	South 南	North 北	South East 東南	East 東	South West 西南	North West 西北	North East 東北	West 西
Xun 巽 4 Wood	North 北	South 南	East 東	South East 東南	North West 西北	South West 西南	West 西	North East 東北
Li 離 9 Fire	East 東	South East 東南	North 北	South 南	North East 東北	West 西	South West 西南	North West 西北

West Group 西宅 Reference Table

Gua 卦	Sheng Qi 生氣	Tian Yi 天醫	Yan Nian 延年	Fu Wei 伏位	Huo Hai 禍害	Wu Gui 五鬼	Liu Sha 六煞	Jue Ming 絕命
Kun 坤 2 Earth	North East 東北	West 西	North West 西北	South West 西南	East 東	South East 東南	South 南	North 北
Qian 乾 6 Metal	West 西	North East 東北	South West 西南	North West 西北	South East 東南	East 東	North 北	South 南
Dui 兌 7 Metal	North West 西北	South West 西南	North East 東北	West 西	North 北	South 南	South East 東南	East 東
Gen 艮 8 Earth	South West 西南	North West 西北	West 西	North East 東北	South 南	North 北	East 東	South East 東南

Problems with using the Life Gua

The Life Gua system is essentially a method of determining an individual person's energy map. You can use the personal auspicious directions to pick a door direction for your house, but that only makes sense, if you are the only person living in the house.

Yes, you see, if you happen to live with other people or family members under one roof, then you'll discover that unless you were all born in the same year or all happen to be part of the East or West group, the auspicious and inauspicious personal directions of each person living in the home will differ. The result is that someone will lose out.

That is not what Feng Shui is all about – the objective is to benefit all the residents of the property, not just one resident. So, the goal should not be to find out which sectors are good for each individual, but which sectors are generally favourable and beneficial to everyone living in the property, collectively. To do this, you need to evaluate the energy map of the house itself.

The House Gua is used to evaluate the property's own energy map. It is based on the sitting direction of the house. Through the House Gua method, we can obtain a basic energy map of the house and thereby determine which are the favourable and unfavourable sectors of the house.

Armed with this information, you can also then determine how well the house uses the good sectors and bad sectors. So for example, you know that Sheng Qi 生氣 (Life Generating) is a good and favourable sector. If you find that the house you are screening has a storeroom or toilet in Sheng Qi 生氣 , then such a house has wasted the good energy areas. So you should probably avoid buying it because you can't use that beneficial space and you don't want to have to renovate. Ideally, you should try to find a house where the good sectors are usable areas. That means those areas are suitable as bedrooms, TV rooms, for locating the Main Door or a study.

When you already have the right rooms in the good sectors, then you can use the Life Gua method to fine-tune the usage of the rooms, through positioning the desk or bed in the most appropriate directions that enable the maximisation of benevolent Qi for the person using the room.

This is of course an extremely simplified overview of how the House Gua and Ming Gua system work together. My aim in this book is to make the information as accurate as possible without being too technical or complicated. The key understanding when it comes to the Ming Gua and House Gua systems in Eight Mansions is that firstly, they are designed to work together, not in isolation and secondly, always bear in mind that personal directions are for fine-tuning the micro approach, not the macro situation.

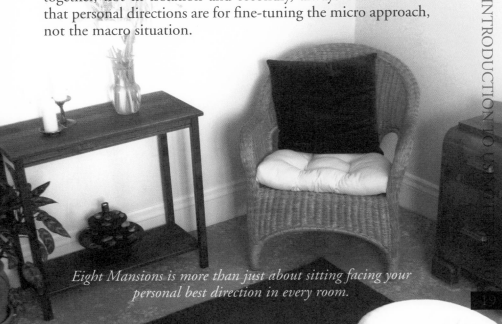

Eight Mansions is more than just about sitting facing your personal best direction in every room.

Interior Feng Shui Essentials

To screen the interior of a house, you need to first learn how to perform some simple measurements and demarcate the interior of a property correctly. This is both to enable you to evaluate the internal forms found in the interior of the property, and also to enable you to undertake some simple formula-based assessment, using the Eight Mansions system. After all, you can't know if a house is facing a favourable direction or unfavourable direction if you don't even know which direction it faces in the first place.

How to Take a Direction

Directions form an integral aspect of applying Feng Shui, whether it is for evaluating the exterior environment or the interior environment. This section will show you how to obtain the Facing Direction of a property.

The first step in taking a direction is to observe the façade of the property. How do you decide what the façade is? The main technique is to observe the direction the house was designed to face. The common mistake when it comes to taking a direction that many people make is to assume that they have to use the Main Door as the reference point. Sometimes, the Main Door is the façade, sometimes it is not. So to be on the safe side, look at the façade.

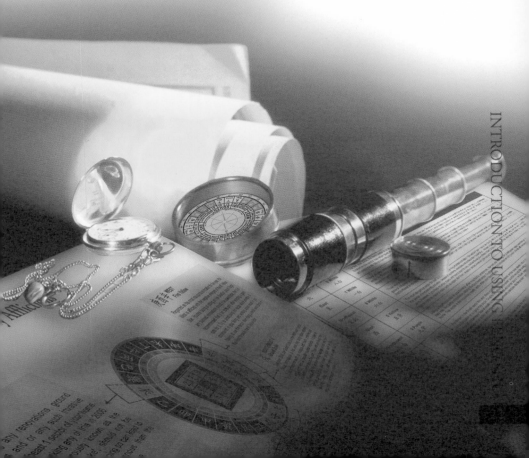

Door Facing + House Facing (Facade)

Don't assume that the Main Door always indicates the Facing of the Property.

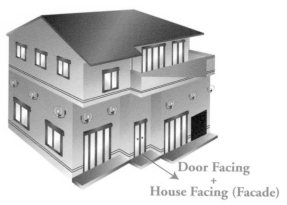

Door Facing
+
House Facing (Facade)

*In this illustration, the Main Door and the Facing
of the property are one and the same direction.*

House Facing (Facade) *Door Facing*

*This illustration shows you an example of when the Main Door
and the Facing of the property are not in the same direction.*

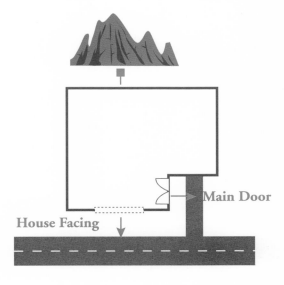

Main Door

House Facing

Once you have identified where the building faces (known as the Facing), stand at the Central Palace (that's Feng Shui terminology for the center of the façade) look out and see what direction the compass yields. That direction gives you the Facing Direction of the property.

It is extremely important not to rely on 'where the sun rises and sets' to obtain the Facing Direction as this can be highly inaccurate. Getting a direction doesn't really require a luo pan but you should at least get a compass (such as an automatic compass or electronic compass) to ensure a reasonably accurate direction reading.

When evaluating exterior Feng Shui and the greater macro environment, the 8 cardinal directions are demarcated. When you are evaluating interior Feng Shui however, the 9 Grid or 9 Palaces method is used. This is because Qi does not have a fixed form. It does not move by borderlines – Qi moves by room size as it can fill a room or contract in a space.

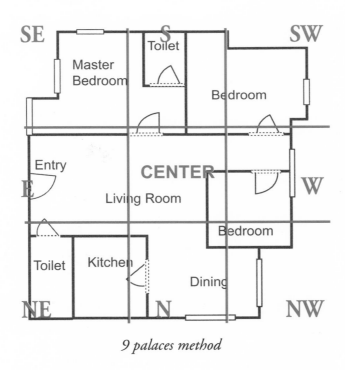

9 palaces method

To demarcate the 9 Palaces in a house, you will need a copy of the house plan. It is preferable to use an architect's drawing of the house plan rather than one you have drawn yourself as this will at least ensure accuracy and correct scaling when it comes to dimensions and room sizes.

Using the 9 Palaces Stencil

Once you have identified the Facing direction of your property, simply place the transparency with the 9 Palaces found at the back of this book over your house plan. Mark out the Facing direction at the center palace of the facing grid. So for example, if your house faces Northwest, then the 9 Palaces in the property would be demarcated as per the illustration below, with Northwest in the center of the Facing Grid. Proceed to then mark the rest of the directions according to the compass directions. There is no direction for the palace right in the center. This is referred to as the Central Palace, Heavenly Heart of the House or the Tai Ji (太極) in Feng Shui.

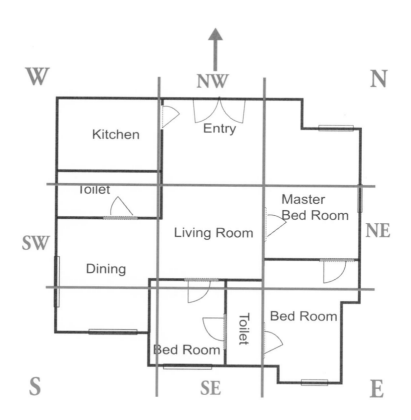

To determine the energy map of the house, you need to know which of the 8 Houses in Eight Mansions Feng Shui corresponds with the property you are screening. Once you have the Facing Direction, simply match the Facing Direction to the appropriate Qi map of the property, based on the reference overleaf. So for example if your house faces South, then you have a Kan Gua house.

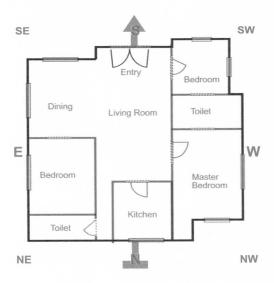

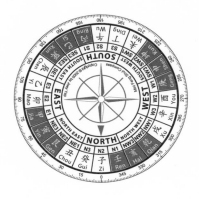

House Facing South (Sitting North)
Kan Gua #1 (water)

Auspicious 吉 ☐   Inauspicious 凶 ☐

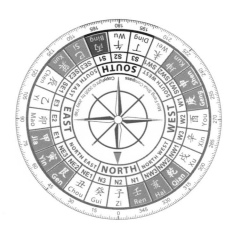

House Facing West (Sitting East)
Zhen Gua #3 (wood)

Auspicious 吉 ☐   **Inauspicious** 凶 ☐

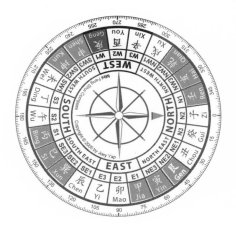

Auspicious 吉 ☐   Inauspicious 凶 ▨

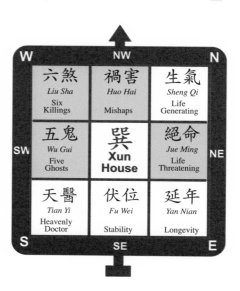

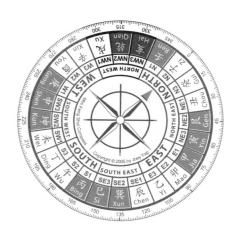

Auspicious 吉 ☐   Inauspicious 凶 ☐

NW	N	NE
絕命 *Jue Ming* Life Threatening	延年 *Yan Nian* Longevity	禍害 *Huo Hai* Mishaps
五鬼 *Wu Gui* Five Ghosts	離 Li **House**	生氣 *Sheng Qi* Life Generating
六煞 *Liu Sha* Six Killings	伏位 *Fu Wei* Stability	天醫 *Tian Yi* Heavenly Doctor

W · E / SW · S · SE

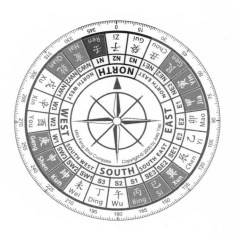

House Facing Northeast (Sitting Southwest)
Kun Gua #2 (earth)

Auspicious 吉 ☐　　　Inauspicious 凶 ☐

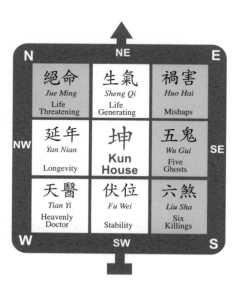

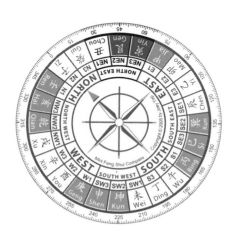

Auspicious 吉 ☐   Inauspicious 凶 ▨

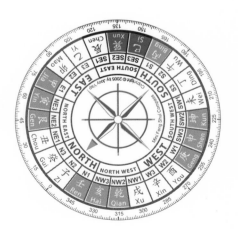

House Facing East (Sitting West)
Dui Gua #7 (metal)

Auspicious 吉 ☐   Inauspicious 凶 ☐

NE	E	SE
延年 *Yan Nian* Longevity	絕命 *Jue Ming* Life Threatening	六煞 *Liu Sha* Six Killings
禍害 *Huo Hai* Mishaps	兌 **Dui House**	五鬼 *Wu Gui* Five Ghosts
生氣 *Sheng Qi* Life Generating	伏位 *Fu Wei* Stability	天醫 *Tian Yi* Heavenly Doctor

(N on left, S on right; NW, W, SW at bottom)

Auspicious 吉 ☐   Inauspicious 凶 ▨

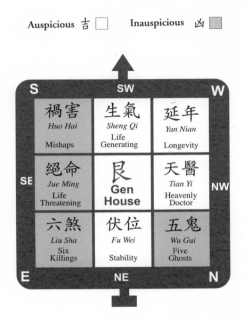

S	**SW**	**W**
禍害 *Huo Hai* Mishaps	生氣 *Sheng Qi* Life Generating	延年 *Yan Nian* Longevity
SE 絕命 *Jue Ming* Life Threatening	艮 **Gen House**	**NW** 天醫 *Tian Yi* Heavenly Doctor
六煞 *Liu Sha* Six Killings	伏位 *Fu Wei* Stability	五鬼 *Wu Gui* Five Ghosts
E	**NE**	**N**

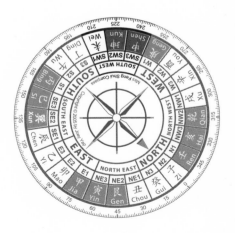

The Eight Types of Qi

Now that you have ascertained which of the Eight Houses in Eight Mansions Feng Shui you are screening or evaluating, you need to understand something about the 8 types of Qi. If you look at the Eight Houses, you will note that each of the eight directional sectors is governed by a type of Qi. Before you can learn how to make use of the Eight sectors, you must first understand what type of Qi governs that area and what it is used for.

Sheng Qi 生氣 (Life Generating)

This is benevolent positive Qi and it governs financial and reputation matters. Sheng Qi is used to help improve wealth opportunities and to help improve authority, status and reputation.

Tian Yi 天醫 (Heavenly Doctor)

Tian Yi Qi helps to strengthen vitality and assist with healing and health. It also brings about help and assistance from Noble People or Mentors.

Yan Nian 延年 (Longevity)

Yan Nian works to help improve relationship luck and help promote and foster relationships and networking. It is also used to help improve communications between parties and individuals.

Fu Wei 伏位 (Stability)

This type of Qi has a calming effect and is usually used for activities such as meditation, self-cultivation or for resting.

Huo Hai 禍害 (Mishaps)

This type of Qi brings problems, disharmony, disunity and hassles but these are usually annoying problems rather than detrimental problems. This type of Qi makes people uneasy.

Wu Gui 五鬼 (Five Ghost)

Wu Gui Qi results in illnesses and general calamity or bad luck, usually relating to financial affairs. It brings about betrayal and fraudulent activities, and can also, in certain instances, result in robbery or theft.

Liu Sha 六煞 (Six Killings)

This type of Qi creates problems due to lawsuits. It also brings about disputes, arguments and conflict. Sometimes, it can also result in bodily harm, caused by conflict or dispute.

Jue Ming 絕命 (Life Endangering)

This type of Qi brings about misfortune including serious health problems, accidents and injuries and sometimes, family or marital break-up.

The Dream House with Negative Direction

Let's say that you have found a house you really like. Everything about it is perfect. Except, the Feng Shui. Perhaps the door is in the Jue Ming 絕命 (Life Endangering) sector or faces your inauspicious direction. Can you still buy the house?

Remember, we don't practice blanket policies in Feng Shui. Rather, houses with such Facing Directions must be utilised correctly and properly, under the guidance of a qualified professional Feng Shui consultant. Since this book is for screening purposes, and the goal is to make it easy and simple for you to screen houses, I have chosen to err on the side of safety and advise avoiding such houses.

If you are very keen to buy the house or it is the only choice on your list, you can buy but only if you are absolutely certain that there are no negative environmental forms internally and externally affecting the property. Since evaluating the forms in the environment thoroughly is beyond the scope of the average person, it is strongly advised that you have a professional Classical Feng Shui consultant audit and evaluate the property before you make a final decision.

If all the immediate forms surrounding the property and within the property are positive, a Jue Ming 絕命 (Life Endangering) door is not dangerous. If the forms are not negative, the house is not necessarily bad. This is because a negative situation based on the formula assessment does not mean the property is condemned or unusable. The environment 'activates' the formulas remember? Thus if the environment is positive, even a negative Jue Ming (Life Endangering) door will not be harmful.

There are several reasons for this. Firstly, a very important component of Feng Shui is time. Every property, at certain times, will be very bad, and very good. Every property, at certain times, will have negative stars at the Main Door and positive stars at the Main Door. In that sense, nothing is truly forever or permanent when it comes to Feng Shui.

Secondly, there is of course the forms factor. Positive forms can help reduce or suppress the problems that may arise from a door in an inauspicious sector or an inauspicious facing direction. Finally, the Star Counter Palace Method, a special Eight Mansions technique, may qualify the situation further and in fact, render the house usable.

I strongly recommend that you seek a professional Classical Feng Shui consultant's advice before putting down money on the property. If you don't want to incur the cost of bringing in a consultant, then it is best to avoid such houses.

Understanding Location vs Direction

In Classical Feng Shui, an important distinction needs to be made between location and direction. This is especially so when it comes to interior Feng Shui. Internally, a house is always divided up into 9 sectors based on the 9 Palaces method. Each sector is a single location. But within each location, you have 360 degrees of directions to face. So for example, a room can be located in the South sector, but the desk faces the West direction. Or the Main Door of the house can be located in the West sector, but the door itself faces East.

Take a look at Picture A. This shows a person sleeping in the West sector of the house, with the bed facing the West direction. In picture B, the bedroom is in the Southwest Sector, but the bed is orientated towards the West. In picture C, the bed is in the Southwest sector, but the bed is orientated towards the South. These three diagrams illustrate the distinction between location and direction.

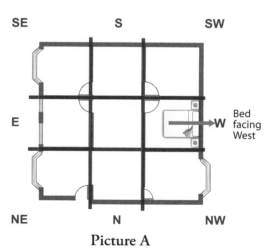

Picture A
Bed located in West room, with headboard facing West direction.

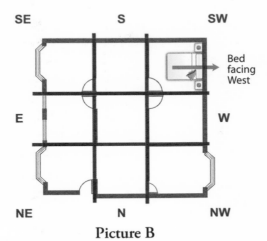

Picture B

*In this diagram, the Bed is located in the Southwest sector,
but the bed headboard is still facing the West direction.*

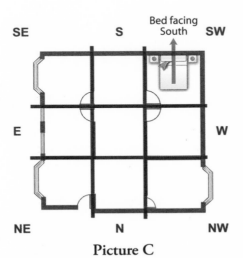

Picture C

*In this diagram, the Bed is located in the Southwest sector,
but the headboard is now facing the South direction.*

How do you know when to use directions and when to use location? It's easy. You use directions when the reference point is your Personal Life Gua or Ming Gua. So if you are trying to fine-tune the facing of your desk or bed, you look at your Life Gua or Ming Gua.

Location on the other hand, refers to common areas that can be used or shared by many people, such as the Main Door, kitchen, TV room or activity room. It is always based on the House Gua. So when you are looking for the best room to locate a bedroom, desk or kitchen, you base it on the House Gua.

Which is more important?

The old real estate mantra 'location, location, location' holds true when it comes to interior Feng Shui as well. It is always better to be in a good location but not necessarily facing your personal favourable direction, than to be in a bad location facing your personal favourable direction. This is because it is better to be in a room that already has good energy, and then enhance or fine-tune it with your own personal favourable direction than be in a room with negative energy. The sector is already diminished in its Qi quality and facing your auspicious or best direction cannot help an already dire situation.

Also, remember that you can face a direction from any location – every room has 360 degrees in theory that you can face. In an ideal world, it is best to be in a good location, and face your own personal best direction.

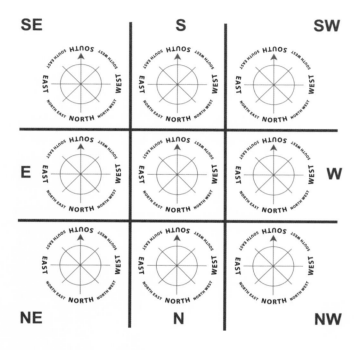

As this diagram illustrates, it is theoretically possible to face your Favourable Direction from any sector in the property. So why not be in a good sector to benefit from the good Qi there while facing that Favourable Direction?

This confusion between location and direction, and the lack of knowledge as to how they rank in priority when it comes to Feng Shui, is the cause of a frequent common mistake many people make when trying to utilise Eight Mansions. That mistake is to base their entire property's Feng Shui, on their personal favourable directions.

As a result, Feng Shui becomes ridiculous to practice because this means East and West group people (people with different personal directions) technically cannot live in the same house and East and West group couples cannot sleep in the same bedroom. It is patently ridiculous to tell a husband and wife that they should not sleep in the same room, or that they should sleep in different directions on the same bed. And frankly, it is just unnecessary.

As I frequently tell students and clients, Feng Shui is a practical science. And most of all, it is a science of common sense. Sleeping in different directions on the same bed, facing your spouse's feet, does not make sense.

Missing Sectors and Protruding Sectors

A property's structure is the container of Qi. Obviously we prefer it to be a complete container although sometimes, some houses have what is termed a 'missing sector'. In other words, the container is not complete.

The 9 sectors in the house represent the Luo Shu map. The Luo Shu in its complete entirety represents a perfect balance of the 5 elements. These 5 elements are the equivalent of the organs in the human body. Thus, a house with all the 5 Elements and 9 Sectors, is a house with complete and vibrant Qi and thus is immune to most negative influences externally as well as the annual negative influences. Missing corners of the house are like a missing organ, thus when something is missing, you are susceptible to certain problems. A protrusion is the opposite of a missing corner – so using the example of a human body, having a protrusion is basically like having two copies of one vital organ.

When does a house have a missing sector?

After drawing the 9 Palace grid over the house plan, if more than 1/3 of any of the horizontal or vertical grid spaces is missing, a house is considered to have a missing sector problem.

House Plan of property.

House Plan with 9 Palace Grid. There is a small missing portion in the Northeast but as this does not constitute more than one palace or 1/3 of the grid, it is not considered a missing sector.

47

In this case, we can see that the Northeast sector is clearly missing and an entire palace or up to 1/3 of the grid is missing. This is considered a property with a missing sector.

It's a bit tricky evaluating whether or not there is a missing sector, especially when it comes to houses with garages or those with additional 'areas' like patios, extensions or conservatories, which are common in Western houses.

In most Malaysian and Singaporean houses, the garage is essentially a roofed area to park your vehicle – hence the garage should not be considered as part of the property. So when we look at the house plan, we do not consider the garage area as part of the house. However, if the garage is attached to the house and walled, as is common in American and European houses, then you can take into consideration the garage area when determining if a property has a missing sector.

However, generally, we don't take into consideration the garage even when it is a walled sector unless the garage is an important living space area – for example, Jeff Bezos started his businesses from the garage. Many famous entrepreneurs worked out of their garages during the start-up phase of their businesses. If you have your office in the garage, then you should consider the garage as an important part of the house. Accordingly, the garage area will form a part of the house plan.

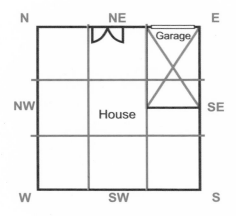

House where the garage is part of the property.

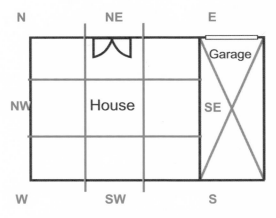

House where garage is not part of the property.

Now, knowing something is missing is one thing, the next issue is to know what the problem is. To know what the problem is, we look to the Trigrams.

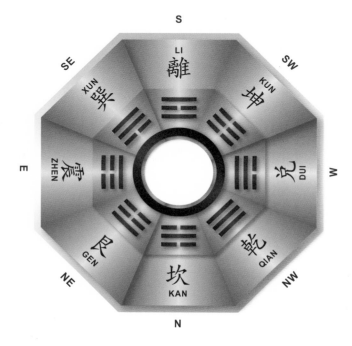

Later Heaven Ba Gua 後天八卦

Each sector in each direction is represented by a Trigram. Trigrams represent the body of energy or Qi in that sector. When a sector is missing or protrudes, we need to know what the impact of such a protrusion or missing sector is to the occupants of the property. To find out what the impact is, we turn to the Trigrams or Gua as it is known as in Chinese.

The Trigrams

The Trigrams are the basis for all interpretations in any school of Feng Shui. In Feng Shui, each directional sector (i.e. North, South, East) is governed by a Trigram. The Trigram represents and illustrates the basic energies and attributes of that area. When a sector of a property is affected by negative forms, or missing/protruding sectors, the Trigram holds the key to unlocking "what" will be affected.

Trigrams can go into tremendous depth and it would not be incorrect to say that everything in the universe probably has a Trigram reference. For example, Dui Gua, which is the Trigram that represents the West sector, can represent a person (a young girl), an animal (Rooster), a certain point of time (Autumn), an object (a knife) or a part of the body (mouth). For basic usage, I have provided you here with a very simple list of basic references for the Trigrams.

Qian 乾 ☰

Element:	Metal.
Number:	6
Direction:	Northwest
People:	The emperor, father, adult, old people, senior person, famous person, emperor's servant, government officer and civil servants, boss, leader, chairman.
Body Parts:	Head, bone, lung.
Sickness:	Head/Brain related disease, lung disease, muscle and bone disease.
Color:	Gold, silver, white.

Kun 坤 ☷

Element:	Earth.
Number:	2
Direction:	Southwest
People:	Mother, step-mother, farmer, villager, people/ crowd, old lady and people with big bellies/fat people.
Body Parts:	Abdomen, spleen, flesh, stomach.
Sickness:	Abdominal disease, stomach disease, poor appetite, indigestion .
Color:	Yellow, black.

Zhen 震 ☳

Element:	Wood.
Number:	3
Direction:	East
People:	Eldest son.
Body Parts:	Foot, liver, hair, voice.
Sickness:	Foot disease, liver disease, worries and shock.
Color:	Dark green and jade green.

Xun 巽 ☴

Element:	Wood.
Number:	4
Direction:	Southeast
People:	Eldest daughter, widow.
Body Parts:	Thigh, Qi and disease of Feng/wind/gas.
Sickness:	Thigh problems, disease of Feng/wind, intestinal disease, stroke and disease of Qi.
Color:	Green, jade green.

Kan 坎 ☵

Element:	Water.
Number:	1
Direction:	North
People:	Middle son, people who are working on the sea/river/lake etc. for example: fisherman, sailor, pirates.
Body Parts:	Ear, blood, kidney.
Sickness:	Ear sickness, infection, kidney and stomach problem, diarrhea.
Color:	Black, blue.

Li 離 ☲

Element:	Fire.
Number:	9
Direction:	South
People:	Middle daughter, writers.
Body Parts:	Eye, heart.
Sickness:	Eye disease, heart disease
Color:	Red, purple.

Gen 艮 ☶

Element:	Earth.
Number:	8
Direction:	Northeast
People:	Youngest son, young kids, people living in the jungle, a hermit or a person who has lots of free time.
Body Parts:	Finger, bone, nose, back, back bone.
Sickness:	Problems of the finger/toes, stomach and back.
Color:	Yellow.

Dui 兑 ☱

Element:	Metal.
Number:	7
Direction:	West
People:	Youngest daughter, mistress, singer, actor.
Body Parts:	Tongue, mouth, throat, lung, phlegm, saliva.
Sickness:	Mouth or tongue disease, throat disease, respiratory disease, lack of appetite.
Color:	White.

As you overlay various levels of formulas, and various levels of Luan Tou 巒頭 (Landform) analysis and techniques, the outcome of the missing sector obviously has greater significance. Of course, the technicalities are not something we shall concern ourselves with here because the goal of this book is to help you make a simple decision as to whether or not the missing corner is acceptable or not.

Do you have a Missing Sector problem?

Before the Trigrams come into the picture, you need to first, make sure that you actually have a missing sector problem. So first, draw the 9 Palace grids over your house plan and check if any of the horizontal or vertical spaces on the grid has up to 1/3 of it missing. Assuming a sector is really missing, then you next need to ask if it is a serious or minor problem.

So, let's take a look at an example. The diagram below shows a house that has a missing South sector. What does South represent in the Trigrams? South is governed by Li Gua and Li Gua governs amongst other things, the middle aged lady, the heart, the eyes, and Fire.

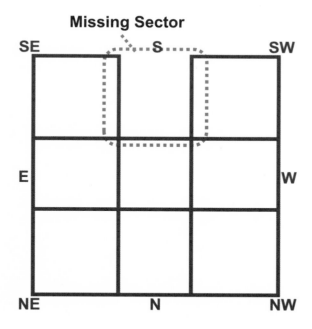

This property has a clear missing sector and the missing sector is South.

Accordingly, if anything negative is to happen, the most susceptible person is anyone who is a middle aged woman. This person will most likely have an eye or heart related problem. Now, Fire in the study of Five Elements represents elegance, passion and mannerisms and thus if a house has a missing South sector, the occupants of the house will likely have issues related to their personal happiness. Of course, knowing the precise outcome requires further investigation, such as looking at the personal Life Gua of the occupants, and of course, the Flying Stars and the timing of the stars. But this example gives you a simple and basic idea of how understanding the Trigrams can help unlock the outcomes of missing sectors.

離 ☲ Li Gua

Element:	Fire.
Number:	9
Direction:	South
People:	Middle daughter, writers.
Body Parts:	Eye, heart.
Sickness:	Eye disease, heart disease
Color:	Red, purple.

The three key internal factors

When it comes to interior Feng Shui, a classical Feng Shui consultant will prioritise the evaluation of three key features of the house: the Main Door, the Kitchen and the Bedroom. These days of course, the consultant will also usually check the study as well, since many people now work from home or bring work home.

When you are screening a house interior, don't get fixated over the colour of the cabinets or the tiles on the floor. Always check the three key internal factors first. Remember, everything else that is good is a bonus, if these three key internal factors are good. Everything else won't bring much benefit if these three key internal factors are negatively affected.

At the end of the day, you want to get these three factors right. That means there are positive forms at the Main Door, in the Kitchen and the Bedroom or there are no negative forms affecting any of the three. Ideally, they should also be located in the right sectors.

Main Door   *Kitchen*   *Bedroom*

The Feng Shui Mindset

People sometimes approach Feng Shui with excessive zeal, to the point where everything can be Feng Shui'ed and every corner has to be 'cured' and 'activated'. I have also met clients who are paranoid of even moving the furniture, for fear that they will upset some delicate balance in the Qi universe as it were.

Applying Feng Shui in your home or property requires neither mindset. Instead, you should approach it in a practical, logical and informed manner. That means not getting paranoid over small things (like a tiny sharp corner) and not going overboard by trying to have the best of everything, and ending up in a house that is uncomfortable or resembles an interior designer's worst nightmare.

First, Feng Shui is about prioritiesjapan 1 is not bad
. Certain factors are more important than others. For example, is it more important to be located in the right room, than it is to be in a bad room but facing your favourable direction. It is more important to have a good Main Door unaffected by negative forms, than it is to have just a good Facing Direction.

Getting a perfect house is really hard and sometimes, can't be achieved no matter how much money the client is willing to throw on renovations. For example, you might have a beam in a room that is creating a negative form like a piercing heart Sha Qi. But you can't remove it because it is a structural beam that holds up your roof!

Secondly, Feng Shui is, contrary to popular misconception, quite a practical science. There is no need to 'cure' every problem in sight and even then, there are ways to implement cures that do not require the placement of unsightly crass objects or involve turning your house into a sort of garish Chinese restaurant with a cure crammed into every nook and cranny. A true master leaves no trace of his presence behind – in a property where the Feng Shui has been well-done, only another professional will be able to see the 'kung fu' of the Master.

In fact, in Feng Shui, if you can avoid or sidestep the problem, then it is better to do that than to cure the situation. So don't be afraid to pass up on a property if it's not right. After all, you wouldn't buy something that's broken in the store, and then spend money fixing it. So why buy a property that is flawed in the first place and then have to spend money just to get it to work?

Never have the mentality that it can be fixed or a sufficiently good Feng Shui practitioner can solve the problem. Remember, not all Feng Shui problems have cures or solutions. Not buying is sometimes the best remedy out there (and it's free!)

Chapter Two:
Forms and the
Main Door

In the first book of this series, ***Feng Shui for Homebuyers – Exterior***, I talked about the importance of observing the features of the environment in and around a piece of property, in order to ascertain if the area fosters benevolent positive Qi or negative Qi. What are these features I'm talking about?

The key features in the exterior environment are of course, Mountains and Water. These two features form the backbone of what is known as Landform Feng Shui or Luan Tou Feng Shui (巒頭風水). I also talked about certain negative environmental features or negative forms that are undesirable in your immediate environment.

Landform Feng Shui also extends to the interior of the property. In Feng Shui, there is such a thing as interior forms. Like external Landform, these are favourable or unfavourable features such as sharp corners or beams within the home or property that either help to collect Qi or repel Qi. These features are ascertained through physical observation - in other words, you need to see if the features are present or not inside the house. For clarity, I will refer to forms in the macro environment as 'exterior forms' or 'external forms' throughout this book, and forms within the inside of the house as 'interior forms' or 'internal forms'.

Always remember that you must first observe the macro environment and the external forms found in that environment (by this I mean the mountains and rivers and other environmental features within a 1-2 km radius of the property in question) before you proceed to evaluate the interior forms.

Think Macro before you go Micro. As far as possible, always check the external environment landforms before looking in the house.

The Main Door

Main Door

After the environment, the Main Door, along with the Kitchen and Bedroom, form part of what are termed the Three Important Factors in Feng Shui. These are the three features of the home that any Classical Feng Shui consultant absolutely must evaluate.

The importance of the Main Door cannot be stressed enough. The Main Door is essentially the Qi mouth of the House. This is the primary entrance for Qi from the environment. Accordingly, it is extremely important that the Main Door is not negatively or adversely affected by forms in any way because this will affect the ability of the property to receive Qi from the environment. A good environment must be accompanied by a good Main Door or you will simply be wasting what is in the environment! Hence, you do not want to see any external (or internal) forms affecting the Main Door that might repel, expel or block Qi, nor do you want any forms that exude Sha Qi 煞 氣 (Killing Qi) to hit your Main Door.

A quick reminder at this juncture: it is important when you are evaluating the interior forms, that you have a clear understanding of the difference between Direction and Location, as explained in Chapter 1. Remember, we are always more concerned about being in the right location, than we are about facing the right direction. Hence you cannot compensate for a bad Main Door by having a good Facing Direction or favourable Flying Stars in the Main Door sector. If the Main Door is negatively affected by internal or external forms, it is a bad Main Door, irrespective of how good the Facing direction of the House is, or how good the Flying Stars at the Main Door sector are.

In contrast, a Main Door that has positive forms can help compensate for a less than favourable Facing direction or help reduce the impact of negative stars when they arrive at the Main Door.

Always look for a home with a good Main Door, surrounded by positive landform.

When evaluating the Main Door, it is important to not just look in, but to look out as well. Often, when people evaluate a house or check a house out, they open the door and look right in. Very few people stand at the Main Door and then look out.

Main Door looking out

Main Door looking in

When it comes to evaluating the Main Door, you need to be aware of the importance of forms that affect the Main Door internally and externally. Internal forms are forms located inside the house and affect the Main Door from the inside, while external forms are forms that affect the Main Door from the outside. I will show you how to evaluate your Main Door in both situations.

It is important not to confuse the Main Door with the Facing of the property. Remember, the Main Door does not necessarily share the Facing of the property. Finally, remember that the "facing direction" of the Main Door is not as important as the "location" of the Main Door. Ideally, the Main Door should be located in a good sector, even if it is not facing the best direction.

Door Facing + House Facing (Facade)

*In this diagram, the door facing and
the house facing are the same direction.*

House Facing (Facade)

Door Facing

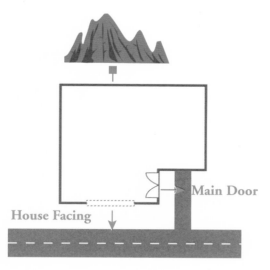

Main Door

House Facing

*The door facing and the house facing in this example are not the
same direction.*

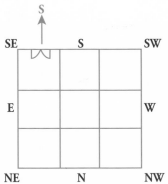

Main Door located in Southeast sector, facing South

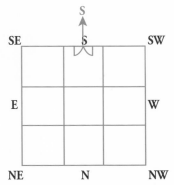

Main Door located in South sector, facing South

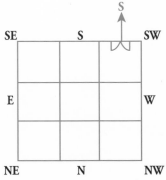

Main Door located in Southwest sector, facing south

*This set of diagrams illustrates the difference between the location
of the Main Door and its Facing Direction.*

FORMS AND THE MAIN DOOR

At The Main Door, Looking Out

In this section, we are concerned with checking for any external forms that may affect the Main Door. Now, as the purpose of this book is to enable you to screen houses, you should not be too concerned with every sharp corner or every possible negative form.

Concentrate on what you can actually SEE from the Main Door. There is no need for any special equipment or to stand on a chair or anything like that. Simply stand at the Main

Door, look out and check that you do not see any of the negative forms discussed here from that position. So do not be paranoid – think proximity! If there is a lamp post visible from your Main Door but it is about 1 km away, you really do not have a problem!

Not every sharp object is a cause for concern - the question is, how far away is it from your property?

When you look out of a house and immediately you spot a lamp post, you have a possible case of Piercing Heart Sha 穿心 煞 on your hands. This applies if you see a pillar or tree or pole of some sorts from the Main Door. Piercing Heart Sha is a big no-no because it not only affects the health of the occupants of the property, but also results in career obstacles.

To verify if it is indeed Piercing Heart Sha, you have to extend an imaginary line from the two sides of the door, out towards the negative feature. If the negative feature is within the boundaries of the Main Door, then you have Piercing Heart Sha. If it is outside the imaginary line, then it is okay.

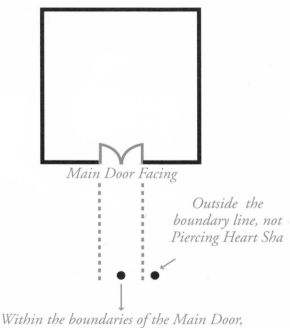

Main Door Facing

Outside the boundary line, not Piercing Heart Sha

Within the boundaries of the Main Door, considered Piercing Heart Sha

When checking for negative forms impacting on your Main Door, always extend an imaginary line from the two sides of the Main Door outwards, and see if the negative form is within that boundary or not. A negative form only affects the Main Door if it is within the boundaries of the door.

Lamp post directly in front of Main Door.

Spacious Bright Hall

This book is not just about the negative features you should look out for. There are also positive features that you should look out for in a home. This book, as I have mentioned in the preface, is about screening houses. That means screening the problematic ones out and screening the good ones in!

The Bright Hall (明堂聚水化萬煞 Ming Tang Ju Shui Hua Wan Sha) is a Feng Shui term that essentially refers to the space directly in front of the property. Let me quickly dispel a few myths about the Bright Hall. It is not your porch light that makes your porch a 'Bright Hall'. Having multiple lights in front of your house also does not create a Bright Hall. The term 'Bright Hall' refers to a spacious area in front of the Main Door that helps to collect Qi in the area. You see, Qi must first settle and collect, before you can receive it. You can't put money in your pocket until you have collected it right? It's the same with Qi. Therefore, it is beneficial for a property to have a spacious area in front of the Main Door to collect Qi.

This property does not have a spacious Bright Hall in front of the Main Door.

These two properties have no Bright Hall in front of the Main Door.

Bright Hall collect Qi

*These two properties have spacious Bright Halls in front of the
Main Door, enabling Qi to collect in front of the house.*

Table Mountain 案山

Known as An Shan 案山 in classical Feng Shui literature, the Table Mountain's purpose is to ensure the beneficial Qi does not escape from the property. You see, in Feng Shui, we are really trying to put into effect just a few simple concepts: find the Qi, ensure it has a place to collect, make sure it can't escape and tap it. It's that simple.

Hence, if you look out from your Main Door and in the far distance there is a hill, and the hill, when observed from the Main Door, is almost the same height as your Main Door, that is a good Table Mountain. The Qi in that property is constantly protected and achievements will come much faster for the occupants. However, when the mountain is obviously taller than the house when observed from the Main Door, then you do not have a table mountain.

Obviously this is not a very exact science; so again, remember that you should use common sense and your own judgment. Using Feng Shui Vision is not about sophisticated tools, or exact measurements – sometimes, simple techniques, like judging the Table Mountain in proximity to your Main Door, is all you need.

Table Mountain at the Qing Tombs in He Bei Province.

*Main Door facing a Table Mountain -
this is a good formation to have outside your house.*

Narrow gap between houses pointing at Main Door

If from the Main Door, looking out, you observe a narrow gap between houses, usually as a result of two houses built close together, you have a mini version of Tian Zhan Sha (天斬煞) (Crack in the Sky Sha). This is a highly undesirable external form and you should avoid selecting any property where this negative form is visible from the Main Door. Any property with Crack in the Sky Sha will experience a magnification of negative effects during certain years, when negative Flying Stars reach the Main Door of the property.

Example of a negative form you do not want to see from your Main Door.

Main Door is very dark or shadowed by a lot of trees

Sometimes, as a result of thick greenery or foliage from trees, the Main Door area is very dark or shadowed. This means sunlight is prevented from reaching the doorstep of the house and creates Yin Sha. Yin Sha is hazardous to the mental health of the residents and so you should avoid properties with these kinds of Main Door.

Main door

*An example of a property with a Yin Sha problem.
The Main Door is barely visible.*

Pillar in front of Main Door 頂心柱

A pillar in front of the Main Door is similar to having a lamp post in front of your Main Door. It obstructs the Qi from entering the property and is also a type of Piercing Heart Sha. You should avoid buying a house with such a feature. Of course, the problem can be fixed - the Main Door can be relocated to another sector or a screen can be strategically placed in front of the pillar to redirect the Qi. However, this will only bring minimal or moderate improvement to the situation because the Bright Hall is affected.

*This Main Door is problematic due to the pillar
right in front of it, creating Piercing Heart Sha.*

It's important to remember that the job of the Feng Shui Master is not to fix everything. All too often, during a consultation, whenever a negative feature is mentioned, clients immediately think: "cure it" or "fix it". You have to remember that not everything is 'fixable' in Feng Shui. If that was the case, no one would ever experience bad Feng Shui ever in this world. Feng Shui operates on the basis that you should avoid a problem in the first place, rather than make your life difficult by trying to fix something you could have avoided in the first place.

Finally, try to remember that just as not every problem in this world has a solution, not every negative feature or phenomenon in Feng Shui can be fixed or cured. Certain problem can't be solved or fixed. It has nothing to do with the skill or professionalism of the Feng Shui consultant. ON the contrary, a good consultant will advise you to avoid the problem, rather than encourage a 'cure' or 'fix' because fixing a problem in Feng Shui is not as easy as plonking some trinket, figurine or drawing in a sector and telling yourself, its blocking the negative Qi!

Remember, if you already have the problem, then you fix it. But the trick is to avoid the problem in the first place. Hey, that's why we brush and floss our teeth! Prevention is better than cure. The purpose of this book is to show you on how to avoid a problem so that you can then utilise a Feng Shui consultation to make your property better!

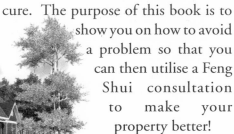

Main Door faces alley

This is a very unfavourable formation and should be avoided at all costs. Qi from the alley is piercing and will hit the Main Door and impede the flow of Qi internally.

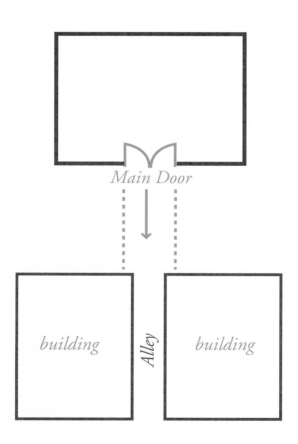

Main Door

building   *Alley*   *building*

*Avoid a property with a Main Door that opens
straight at an alley, like in this picture.*

Main Door faces main gate

Whether or not this poses a problem depends largely on the proximity of the gate to the Main Door. If the gate is very close to the Main Door, then the Qi is rushing too quickly towards the Main Door, especially when the car comes into the house. This is a formation that should be avoided. Qi should always move in a sentimental, meandering manner, not gush aggressively. Of course, this is one of those 'fixable problems' – the easiest solution is to place Water in a strategic location. Water acts as a barrier to Negative Qi and also helps slow down and pacify aggressive Qi.

Main Door faces main gate

If you stand at the Main Door and you immediately see the sharp corner of your opposite neighbour's roof pointing at your door, you have a problem of Fire Sha. Fire Sha causes mishaps, loss of wealth and disharmony in the house. However, this is only the case when the roof is within the frame of the Main Door. How do you check if you have a problem?

Stand at the Main Door and look out normally. If at eye level, you can see a sharp roof pointing right at the Main Door, the property has a Fire Sha problem. However, if the roof is at a higher level (for example, the Main Door is at ground level, whilst the roof is on the 2nd floor) then this is not a problem as you would not be able to perceive the Fire Sha standing at the Main Door.

*If you can see your neighbour's sharp roof from the Main Door,
then Sha Qi is being directed at the Main Door.*

Main Door faces T-junction road

The notorious T-junction has a bad reputation. Even non-believers in Feng Shui know this one and avoid houses near the T-junction by instinct. The truth is, you only need to be concerned if the Main Door itself is hit by the T-junction. What do I mean by 'hit' by the T-junction? This means if you draw an imaginary extension of the road from the T-junction towards the property, and that road leads straight to the Main Door, the Main Door is considered 'hit' by the T-junction. If the T-junction is not within the radius of the Main Door, then the T-junction does not 'hit' the Main Door and you can usually alleviate any negative effects by planting trees or plants to create a barrier for the negative Qi, build a wall or fence or place Water in certain locations.

Assuming the T-junction does hit the Main Door, the severity of the problem really depends on the traffic at the T-junction. If the traffic is heavy, the Crashing Sha is a serious problem and may bring about serious and severe health problems or accidents, which can be fatal, depending again on the Flying Star chart of the property and the Gua that is affected. Now, this situation can be fixed but is very difficult to do; so it is best to avoid it.

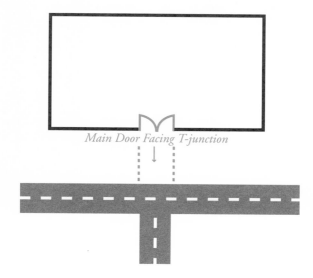

Main Door Facing T-junction

Main Door faces
T-junction road

*A T-junction is not always bad. The question to ask is,
does it affect the Main Door?*

Main Door faces a Ba Gua mirror

Contrary to popular misconception, this is totally harmless. The Ba Gua mirror mainly causes psychological effects because people often associate it with hexing or ghosts or reflecting bad Qi. It has absolutely no bad Feng Shui effect and if you have a house that has a Main Door that looks straight at a Ba Gua Mirror, don't be worried. Check for the real negative features instead!

Sharp pointy edges are regarded as Sha Qi, which is aggressive, destructive and disruptive to the flow of Qi. The edge of a building is considered a form of Sha Qi, known as Edge Sha. This kind of Sha Qi will affect the quality of Qi entering the Main Door. It impedes positive Qi from entering the house. Hence, it is best to avoid a property with a Main Door that has an Edge Sha problem.

This Main Door has Edge Sha affecting it, as a result of the pointy corner from the house opposite.

Main Door sees parallel running drain

If there is a drain that runs parallel to your Main Door, then you may have a problem known as Cutting Feet Water 割 脚水 . In this situation, Water blocks the Qi from entering the property and also cuts into the vitality of the Qi in the house. This is a very negative feature and should be avoided at all costs. Now, you might be thinking, but every house has a drain running outside the house surely? Observe carefully and you will find that this is not a problem for every house. Also, remember that you only have a Cutting Feet Water problem if the drain is VISIBLE from the Main Door. If it is present outside but not visible from the Main Door, you don't have a problem of Cutting Feet Water.

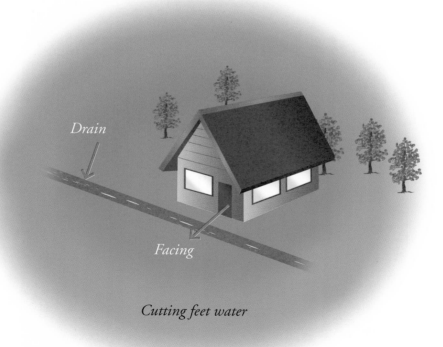

Drain

Facing

Cutting feet water

The proximity between the Main Door and the pond or body of water is the main consideration when you have this kind of formation. If there is ample distance (again, exercise common sense here), then it's not a problem although this may be qualified by the location of the water - a Feng Shui consultant will need to check to see if the direction is suitable for receiving water. If it is, then the water is not just okay, it is actually highly beneficial and the Main Door is a good Main Door that receives prosperous Qi into the house. The main thing you must watch out for is when water is near, rather than far. If the pond or body of water is too close, then there is too much water and Qi is prevented from circulating.

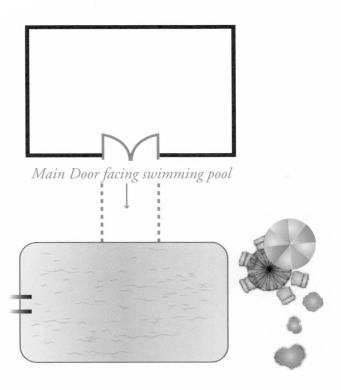

Main Door facing swimming pool

Main Door faces two trees

Ancient Feng Shui texts are often written in highly poetic language – often, the old texts try to sum up a concept in 4 characters or 8 characters, and usually rhyming characters! Sometimes, this causes problem in modern day interpretation because people interpret these old texts literally. This is the case with the formation where the Main Door faces two trees (essentially, a tree which has a fork or where the base branches into a Y shape), which is sometimes called a 'Break Up Tree'.

In the old days, this formation was described to laypersons as a tree that causes the family to split up and go separate ways, hence the term 'Break Up Tree'. The old texts used the term 'Break Up Tree' largely because it rhymed with the first half of the saying. Technically, the reason why a Y shaped tree or forked tree causes this effect is the tree produces Sha Qi that affects the property's people and wealth luck. The gap in the trees directs Sha Qi at the Main Door. Accordingly, if you see such a tree when standing at the Main Door, looking out, you should avoid this property unless you are able to get the tree removed legally.

*The Y-shaped tree is clearly within the imaginary boundaries
of the Main Door, hence, it is clear this Main Door is affected
by the Sha Qi caused by the Y-shaped tree.*

Sliding door vs normal door

This is a popular question I get: does the type of Main Door make a difference? The answer is no. We are not interested in whether the door is a normal type of door or a sliding door, glass door, door that opens inwards or door that opens outwards. Remember, when it comes to the Main Door, it is the direction, location and its ability to receive positive Qi that matters.

Sliding door

Normal door

Tilted Main Door

A tilted Main Door is essentially like a slanted mouth on a face and is not desirable unless the tilting is to tap into certain environmental features. Even then, it is extremely rare for Feng Shui masters to recommend door tilting because the tilting may end up creating Edge Sha or Sha Qi within the immediate area of the Main Door and the owner ends up with a problem that wasn't there in the first place. Most of the time, door tilting is the absolute last resort utilised by a Feng Shui master in extremely dire situations and circumstances. You should be extremely careful of any property where the door has been tilted, especially if the tilting is for Feng Shui reasons. If possible, have the tilt verified by proper Feng Shui master. If you don't have this option, then avoid selecting this property.

Tilted Main Door

Tilted Main Door

*Always be careful when you encounter a tilted Main Door
in a property. It doesn't always mean good Feng Shui.*

At the Main Door, Looking In

After you have stood at the Main Door and looked out, you must now, reverse your position, and look in. Look into the property and observe the features in the immediate vicinity of the Main Door. This area is important because it is here that the Qi will come into first contact with the interior of your property and we want to make sure that it can collect and circulate.

Remember, a Main Door with a good direction is pointless if negative features immediately after the Main Door act to block, repel or squeeze out the Qi.

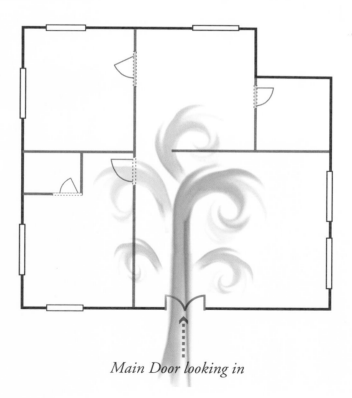

Main Door looking in

When looking in from the Main Door, we are concerned with any forms that might repel or block Qi from entering the property.

Looking in

Toilet in front of Main Door
(looking in)

If you see the door to the toilet the minute you look in, this is not dangerous or bad luck. It simply means all the Qi that enters the home immediately goes into the toilet. This has nothing to do with bad luck being flushed down the toilet. Rather, it just means that all the good Qi is wasted because it ends up residing in the toilet, a room which no one actually uses for more than 10 minutes a day!

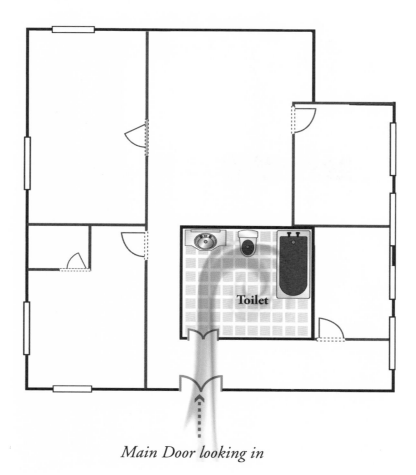

Toilet

Main Door looking in

*Qi entering the Main Door is 'wasted' because it goes
straight into the toilet.*

Mirror in front of Main Door
(looking in)

It is a myth that having a mirror in front of the Main Door is a negative feature. Yes, there may be some psychological impact – people may be surprised by or shocked when they open the door to see themselves in the mirror! It is for this reason that having a mirror in front of the Main Door is not advisable. But in the context of Feng Shui, it has no real Qi effect at all. If you like it there, then fine. If you don't like it, if you feel it is a taboo, then don't put it there.

You might be wondering, where on earth did this idea about the mirror reflecting Qi come from? In the old days, mirrors were not made of glass, but made from brass. Ancient texts refer to it as using the mirror to steal water or bring in Water (Qi) into the house. The reflection of the water outside is 'brought in' to the house via the mirror. The real explanation is a little more scientific. Because in the old days mirrors were made of brass, this was a Metal element object. Metal, in the study of the Five Elements, produces or attracts the Water element. Hence, the mirror was placed at the front door.

Main Door looking in

There's nothing wrong with a Main Door that
opens to a mirror in the hallway.

Back door visible from Main Door
(looking in)

Classic Victorian houses often have a feature where the minute you open the front door, you see the back door or the back door and front door of the house are linked via a straight through passageway. Such arrangements do not allow Qi to circulate through the house - this type of Qi circulation is called Wu Qing (無情). Qi is not sentimental and does not circulate the house. In layman terms, the wealth escapes the house immediately. Hence, avoid such properties.

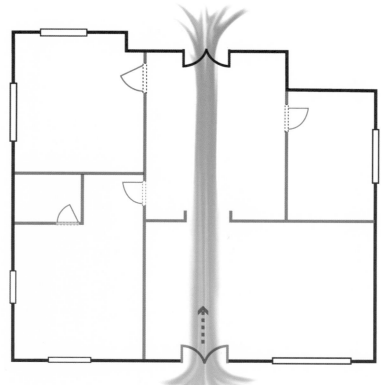

Main Door looking in

*Avoid a property where the Main Door is in direct alignment
with the back door. Qi will just rush in and out of the property
and not collect in the property.*

Another door to another room visible from Main Door (looking in)

Sometimes, the Main Door opens straight to a storeroom or to another room. This means it is this room that receives all the Qi coming through the Main Door. It is considered a disadvantaged or undesirable design as the Qi cannot circulate the house and is trapped inside the room immediately in front of the Main Door.

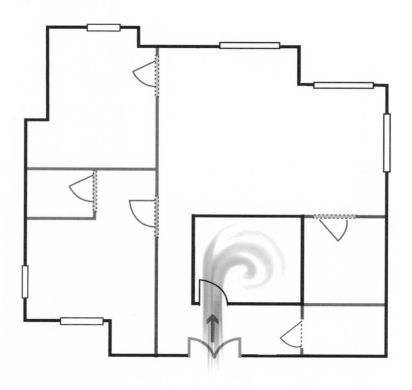

Main Door looking in

*A Main Door opening straight into another room means there's
no chance for Qi to collect and circulate.*

Stairs in front of Main Door (looking in)

In some houses, especially those in Europe, the Main Door immediately opens to a staircase. The Qi gushes down the staircase, combating and repelling the Qi entering the house. Now, you only need to be concerned if the staircase is within 5 feet of the main door but it could be less if the house is very small. If the staircase is far from the door (i.e. more than 8 feet away) it is fine.

As Qi cannot collect and circulate in this type of house, there will be less harmony and vitality in this type of house.

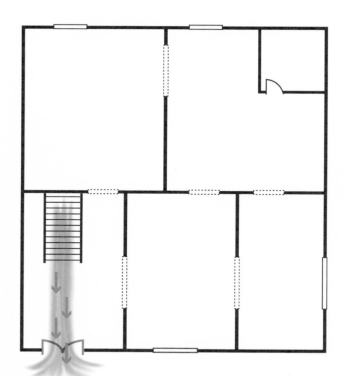

Main Door looking in

Generally, a staircase in front of the Main Door is not a positive formation but always look at the proximity between the staircase and the Main Door first.

Pillar in front of Main Door頂心柱
(looking in)

A pillar right in front of the Main Door blocks Qi from entering the property and circulating inside the house. This is an extremely negative feature within the home. It does not matter if your Main Door faces an excellent direction - you will not be able to get any of the benefits of the good direction with such an internal form affecting the Main Door.

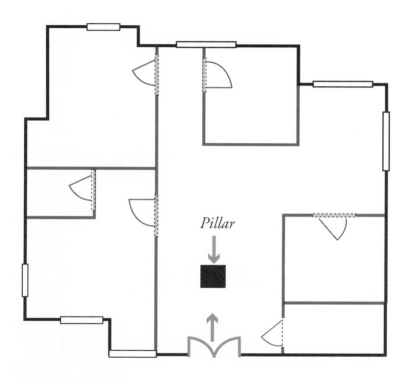

Pillar

Main Door looking in

*This is an example of internal Piercing Heart Sha - this pillar is
splitting the Qi that enters the Main Door.*

Bright Hall 明堂

Feng Shui is about the external and internal and ideally, having the micro of the property reflect what is in the macro of the property. A property therefore should not only have an external Bright Hall, but an internal Bright Hall as well. An internal Bright Hall is essential to the collection of Qi INSIDE your house, just as an external Bright Hall is essential to the collection of Qi within your property, from the environment.

The internal Bright Hall is the space immediately after the Main Door. A spacious area here is needed for Qi to collect and circulate. You cannot make a Bright Hall by putting lights in this area. The only way to have a Bright Hall is to ensure the immediate area in front of the Main Door, looking in, is clear, spacious and broad.

Entry   *Bright Hall*

*Qi needs to collect inside the house hence the need for a Bright
Hall within the immediate interior of the property.*

Beam on top of Main Door

A beam at the top of the Main Door is a classic example of Qi being squeezed out of the house. As the beam exerts pressure on the Main Door, Qi not only does not enter, but gets squeezed out. Avoid buying any property with such a negative internal feature.

Beam

Some houses have a room or a dining hall wall where the corner of the wall is angled directly at the Main Door. This is internal Sha Qi directed at the Main Door. Fixing this is not difficult: simply ask your interior designer to extend the wall all the way to the end. But if you don't want the hassle, avoid picking a property with this feature.

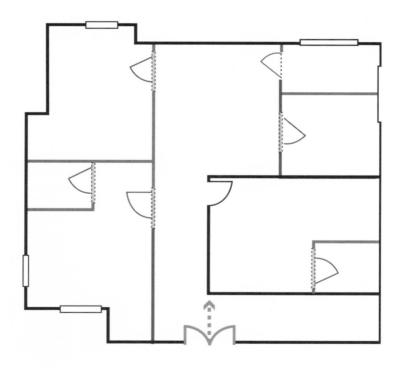

Main Door looking in

*A sharp corner pointing at the Main Door from inside the
house is an example of a negative interior form affecting the
Main Door from the inside.*

Dark Interior

Sometimes, when you enter the Main Door, the immediate area inside the home feels damp, dark, gloomy and musty. This indicates the area near the Main Door is overly Yin and the Yin Qi is too strong. It usually denotes illness in the house. Usually this is a problem caused by the exterior section of the house, just outside the Main Door, also being too Yin. The solution is not easy: the design of the house must be adjusted and changed to enable more natural light to enter the property. It is best not to take a chance with such a property because you may find you cannot solve the problem through renovation.

Chapter Three: Kitchen Forms

After the Main Door, the two most important factors that a Classical Feng Shui consultant will evaluate are the Kitchen and the Bedrooms. In this chapter, I will discuss internal forms that apply to the Kitchen.

Why is the kitchen so important? It is in the kitchen that the food that we eat is prepared. Accordingly, if the Qi in the kitchen is bad, then the residents of the property do not consume good food or proper food, resulting in bad health.

A wrongly or badly located kitchen usually denotes poor health or shortened lifespan for the occupants. The residents have consistent poor health.

In this chapter, I will talk about what are the types of forms that you do not want to see in a kitchen, and then delve briefly into the suitable sectors for a kitchen, using formula-based assessment methods. As always, you should observe the forms first, before you embark on the formula-based assessment because if the forms are negative, locating the kitchen in the appropriate sector is a zero sum gain. Remember, first make sure the forms are good, before you worry about whether the kitchen is located in the right sector.

Now, whenever we talk about the kitchen in Feng Shui, aside from the forms and sector or palace that the kitchen itself is located, we are also concerned with the placement of the stove, as that is the actual device used to cook your food.

Kitchen in center of house

The kitchen should never be located in the central palace or the Heavenly Heart of the property. The central palace is a passive sector of the home, where Qi flow should be subtle and peaceful. Having the kitchen here is like burning the heart of the house it creates instability, long-term and niggling health issues or problems. Remember, the kitchen should always be in one of the side sectors of the house, never the center.

Avoid having the Kitchen in the Central Palace of the house.

Kitchen sink next to stove

In the kitchen, we do not like to have Fire and Water clashing (Shui Huo Xiang Chong 水火相沖). Along the way, this principle seems to have, like so many principles of Feng Shui, developed a life and legend of its own. Let's face it, which kitchen does not have a stove and a sink? The main thing you should be concerned about is the distance between the sink and the stove. As long as there is a gap of 1-2 feet between the stove and the sink, you do not have a problem of fire and water clashing.

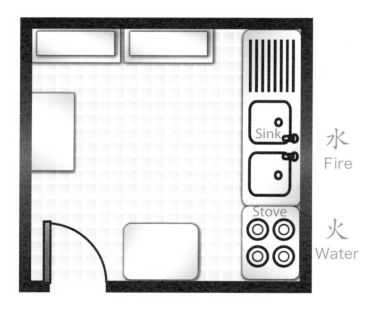

Sink and stove next to each other
in a kitchen.

You should be concerned if the sink and the stove are directly opposite each other. This situation is clearly a case of Fire and Water clashing and the health of the residents will be affected. But even if you do come across a kitchen with this set-up, it's easy enough to solve. Put a console or island between the two, and the clash is averted!

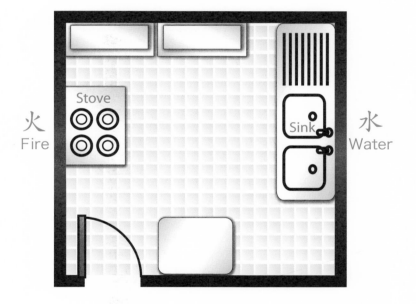

In this kitchen layout, Water and Fire are clearly clashing as the sink and stove are directly opposite each other.

Stove on island in the kitchen

Having an island in the kitchen is a very popular kitchen design these days and it is quite common, especially in western houses, to have the stove on the island portion of the kitchen. Unfortunately, as much as it looks nice, it's not a favourable place to place your stove here in Feng Shui. The stove must always be kept stable and placing it at the centre of the kitchen exposes the stove to Qi from all angles. The food that you cook is affected and so health is a problem. The stove must always be located against a wall, for stability.

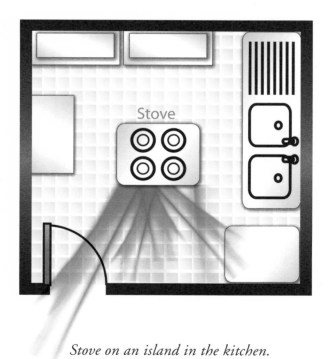

Stove on an island in the kitchen.

Avoid having the stove on the island in the kitchen.

Stove in front of kitchen door
(or any door)

Make sure that your stove is not located in front of any door used to enter the kitchen. This is like a mini T-junction. The Qi from the door rushes in and hits the stove, causing the food that is cooked on the stove to be afflicted with Sha Qi. This situation cannot be rectified simply because the stove is facing the right direction or located in the correct sector in the kitchen. The solution of course is simple – move the stove.

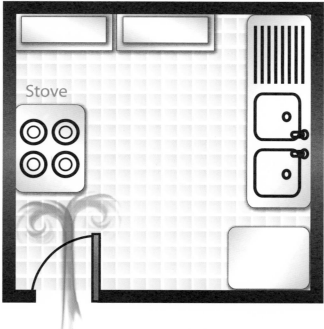

Stove in front of the kitchen door.

Avoid having the stove directly opposite the kitchen door.

Suppressive Qi from the beam above causes a fluctuation of Qi and the stove will be violently affected. This is not a good place to locate your stove. The solution of course is simple enough - move the stove to another location.

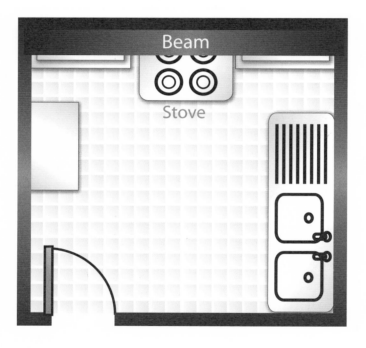

Stove below a beam in the kitchen.

The stove should never be located under a beam in the kitchen.

Stove next to Refrigerator

The problem of Fire and Water clashing has unfortunately, been extended to apply to everything, from the kitchen sink, to the refrigerator. Just because the refridgerator is cold, does not mean it is filled with water! Having your stove next to a refrigerator is NOT a case of Fire and Water clashing so if you have this set-up in your house, it is not a problem.

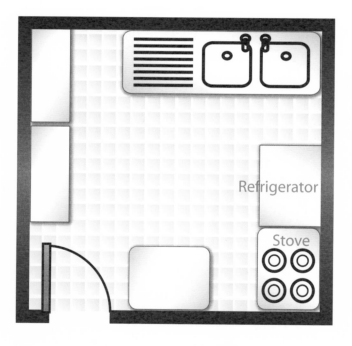

Stove next to refrigerator.

It is ok to put your stove next to the refrigerator in your kitchen.

I want to just briefly dispel some of the misconceptions that people have about their kitchens and Feng Shui. Now, while the Kitchen is one of the three most important factors when it comes to the Feng Shui of the property, that does not mean that you have to treat it like a fragile Ming vase. Forms have an impact on your Kitchen but superstition, old wives tales and urban legends do not!

Displaying knives in your kitchen in a knife block, or using a magnetised knife block, is not harmful or bad Feng Shui or Sha Qi.

Putting coins inside the rice urn, while perhaps it has some symbolic meaning, has absolutely nothing to do with Feng Shui. No, it does not assure abundance or anything like that. It is just a bunch of coins in your rice urn.

Finally, while it is true that we do not like to have water near the stove in the kitchen, that principle does not mean you cannot have a blue kitchen, or blue kitchen cabinets, or use blue tiles. Have the kitchen cabinet, or walls or tiles any colour you like or which is practical for you!

Have your kitchen cabinets whatever colour appeals to you personally.

131

Now that you know the forms in relation to the kitchen, we can look at the ideal situation, where in the kitchen location also matches the formula. Do remember that not all houses are perfect and finding a perfect house is difficult.

The ideal position for the kitchen is usually evaluated using formulas such as the House Gua system in Eight Mansions Feng Shui. The objective is to calculate the most suitable sector for the kitchen. However, the forms, are still relevant. Locating the kitchen in the right sector is pointless if the forms violate the key principles discussed in the previous section on Kitchen Forms.

FENG SHUI FOR HOMEBUYERS - INTERIOR

The kitchen should be located in a negative sector of the house, based on the House Gua. Why is the kitchen located in a negative sector? According to the ancient classics on Eight Mansions Feng Shui, the purpose of locating the kitchen in a negative sector is to suppress the negative Qi in the property.

So let's take a look at an example. This house is a Li Gua House. The negative sectors of the house have been marked in red, for easy reference.

Li Gua #9 (fire)
House facing North (sitting South)

Now, if you find you have a Li Gua house, you should ideally locate your kitchen in any of the negative sectors marked in the diagrams below.

Auspicious 吉 ☐   Inauspicious 凶 ☐

Now, here's a trade secret: your kitchen can be located in a negative sector, but your kitchen stove, or Firemouth, must tap into a favourable direction.

Kitchens and the Life Gua method

The location of the kitchen is always based on the House Gua, not the Life Gua. There's really a logical explanation for this. Using the Life Gua to determine the location of the kitchen, creates silly and contradictory situations. For instance, if the house consists of individuals from both East and West group, then someone has to make a sacrifice. The kitchen will invariably have to be located in SOMEONE's good sector.

For example, a Life Gua 7 and Life Gua 9 couple live in a house. For ease of reference, I have included their Favourable and Unfavourable Directions below.

東命
East Group

Gua 卦	Sheng Qi 生氣	Tian Yi 天醫	Yan Nian 延年	Fu Wei 伏位	Huo Hai 禍害	Wu Gui 五鬼	Liu Sha 六煞	Jue Ming 絕命
Kan 坎 **1 Water**	東南 South East	東 East	南 South	北 North	西 West	東北 North East	西北 North West	西南 South West
Zhen 震 **3 Wood**	南 South	北 North	東南 South East	東 East	西南 South West	西北 North West	東北 North East	西 West
Xun 巽 **4 Wood**	北 North	南 South	東 East	東南 South East	西北 North West	西南 South West	西 West	東北 North East
Li 離 **9 Fire**	東 East	東南 South East	北 North	南 South	東北 North East	西 West	西南 South West	西北 North West

西命
West Group

Gua 卦	Sheng Qi 生氣	Tian Yi 天醫	Yan Nian 延年	Fu Wei 伏位	Huo Hai 禍害	Wu Gui 五鬼	Liu Sha 六煞	Jue Ming 絕命
Kun 坤 **2 Earth**	東北 North East	西 West	西北 North West	西南 South West	東 East	東南 South East	南 South	北 North
Qian 乾 **6 Metal**	西 West	東北 North East	西南 South West	西北 North West	東南 South East	東 East	北 North	南 South
Dui 兑 **7 Metal**	西北 North West	西南 South West	東北 North East	西 West	北 North	南 South	東南 South East	東 East
Gen 艮 **8 Earth**	西南 South West	西北 North West	西 West	東北 North East	南 South	北 North	東 East	東南 South East

Life Gua 7's Jue Ming 絕命 or most unfavourable direction is East. If you make use of the Life Gua method to determine the kitchen placement, then Life Gua 7 should place their kitchen in the East sector to suppress the Jue Ming. But hang on – that means that you are also destroying or suppressing the Sheng Qi 生氣 (the most favourable) location in the house for the Gua 9 person, which happens to be in the East.

This is a highly illogical situation, which technically can only be solved by having two kitchens and even then, this still has the outcome of 'killing off' the positive Qi for each of the occupants somehow.

KITCHEN FORMS

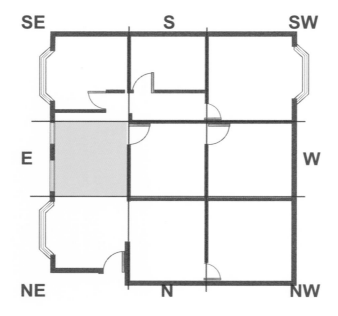

This type of illogical situation is a case of misunderstanding the difference between the Life Gua method and the House Gua method and which method should be used for what. That is quite a technical discussion, and is best reserved for my book on Eight Mansions Feng Shui.

For now, and for the purposes of screening houses, always remember, when determining where to locate important rooms such as kitchens, bedroom and study, follow the House Gua. This way, you are selecting the positive or negative areas of the house, thus providing a positive effect for all the residents. The Life Gua system should be used for personal fine-tuning of directions and is not for placement of rooms.

Kitchen in the Four Negative Sectors

I have included this section for readers who have some familiarity with Eight Mansions and who would like to be able to include a measure of formula-based assessment into their screening of a property. Remember that the House Gua is based on the Sitting of the property – refer to Chapter 1 if you're not sure how to ascertain the House Gua.

East Group 東宅 Reference Table

Gua 卦	Sheng Qi 生氣	Tian Yi 天醫	Yan Nian 延年	Fu Wei 伏位	Huo Hai 禍害	Wu Gui 五鬼	Liu Sha 六煞	Jue Ming 絕命
Kan 坎 1 Water	South East 東南	East 東	South 南	North 北	West 西	North East 東北	North West 西北	South West 西南
Zhen 震 3 Wood	South 南	North 北	South East 東南	East 東	South West 西南	North West 西北	North East 東北	West 西
Xun 巽 4 Wood	North 北	South 南	East 東	South East 東南	North West 西北	South West 西南	West 西	North East 東北
Li 離 9 Fire	East 東	South East 東南	North 北	South 南	North East 東北	West 西	South West 西南	North West 西北

West Group 西宅 Reference Table

Gua 卦	Sheng Qi 生氣	Tian Yi 天醫	Yan Nian 延年	Fu Wei 伏位	Huo Hai 禍害	Wu Gui 五鬼	Liu Sha 六煞	Jue Ming 絕命
Kun 坤 2 Earth	North East 東北	West 西	North West 西北	South West 西南	East 東	South East 東南	South 南	North 北
Qian 乾 6 Metal	West 西	North East 東北	South West 西南	North West 西北	South East 東南	East 東	North 北	South 南
Dui 兌 7 Metal	North West 西北	South West 西南	North East 東北	West 西	North 北	South 南	South East 東南	East 東
Gen 艮 8 Earth	South West 西南	North West 西北	West 西	North East 東北	South 南	North 北	East 東	South East 東南

Kitchen in Jue Ming
絕命 (Life Threatening)

Jue Ming 絕命 is one of the most negative stars in Eight Mansions. Having a kitchen suppressing the Jue Ming star will help you minimise the impact of fatal accidents, mishaps and diseases. However, the Firemouth must tap to a favourable direction such as Tian Yi 天醫 (Heavenly Doctor).

House Facing South (Sitting North)

SE	S	SW
生氣 *Sheng Qi* Life Generating	延年 *Yan Nian* Longevity	絕命 *Jue Ming* Life Threatening
E 天醫 *Tian Yi* Heavenly Doctor	坎 **Kan House**	禍害 *Huo Hai* Mishaps W
五鬼 *Wu Gui* Five Ghosts	伏位 *Fu Wei* Stability	六煞 *Liu Sha* Six Killings
NE	N	NW

Auspicious 吉 ☐
Inauspicious 凶 ▢

SE	S	SW
延年 *Yan Nian* Longevity	生氣 *Sheng Qi* Life Generating	禍害 *Huo Hai* Mishaps
伏位 *Fu Wei* Stability	震 **Zhen House**	絕命 *Jue Ming* Life Threatening
六煞 *Liu Sha* Six Killings	天醫 *Tian Yi* Heavenly Doctor	五鬼 *Wu Gui* Five Ghosts
NE	N	NW

E ← → W

Auspicious 吉 □
Inauspicious 凶 ▨

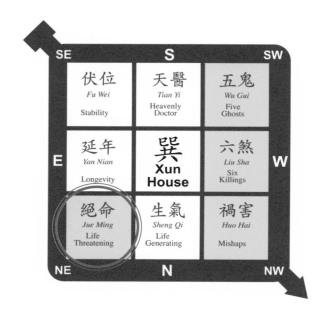

SE	**S**	**SW**
伏位 *Fu Wei* Stability	天醫 *Tian Yi* Heavenly Doctor	五鬼 *Wu Gui* Five Ghosts
延年 *Yan Nian* Longevity	巽 **Xun** **House**	六煞 *Liu Sha* Six Killings
絕命 *Jue Ming* Life Threatening	生氣 *Sheng Qi* Life Generating	禍害 *Huo Hai* Mishaps
NE	**N**	**NW**

Auspicious 吉 ☐
Inauspicious 凶 ▨

House Facing North (Sitting South)

SE	S	SW
天醫 *Tian Yi* Heavenly Doctor	伏位 *Fu Wei* Stability	六煞 *Liu Sha* Six Killings
生氣 *Sheng Qi* Life Generating	離 **Li** **House**	五鬼 *Wu Gui* Five Ghosts
禍害 *Huo Hai* Mishaps	延年 *Yan Nian* Longevity	絕命 *Jue Ming* Life Threatening
NE	N	NW

Auspicious 吉 ☐

Inauspicious 凶 ☐

SE	S	SW
五鬼 *Wu Gui* Five Ghosts	六煞 *Liu Sha* Six Killings	伏位 *Fu Wei* Stability
禍害 *Huo Hai* Mishaps	坤 **Kun House**	天醫 *Tian Yi* Heavenly Doctor
生氣 *Sheng Qi* Life Generating	絕命 *Jue Ming* Life Threatening	延年 *Yan Nian* Longevity
NE	N	NW

Auspicious 吉 ☐

Inauspicious 凶 ▧

SE	**S**	**SW**
禍害 *Huo Hai* Mishaps	絕命 *Jue Ming* Life Threatening	延年 *Yan Nian* Longevity
E 五鬼 *Wu Gui* Five Ghosts	乾 **Qian House**	生氣 *Sheng Qi* Life Generating **W**
天醫 *Tian Yi* Heavenly Doctor	六煞 *Liu Sha* Six Killings	伏位 *Fu Wei* Stability
NE	**N**	**NW**

Auspicious 吉 ☐

Inauspicious 凶 ▨

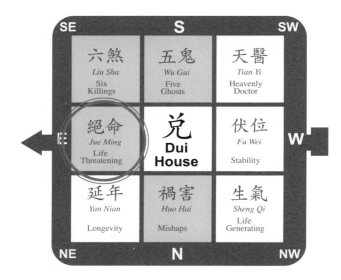

Auspicious 吉 ☐

Inauspicious 凶 ▨

House Facing Southwest (Sitting Northeast)

SE	**S**	**SW**
絕命 *Jue Ming* Life Threatening	禍害 *Huo Hai* Mishaps	生氣 *Sheng Qi* Life Generating
E 六煞 *Liu Sha* Six Killings	艮 **Gen House**	延年 *Yan Nian* Longevity **W**
伏位 *Fu Wei* Stability	五鬼 *Wu Gui* Five Ghosts	天醫 *Tian Yi* Heavenly Doctor
NE	**N**	**NW**

Auspicious 吉 ☐
Inauspicious 凶 ▨

Kitchen in Liu Sha 六煞 (Six Killings)

Liu Sha 六煞 represents legal problems, hassles, bodily harm and severe injury or surgery. People who have a Liu Sha problem invariably find they encounter frequent betrayal, robbery, sports injuries and nicks and cuts. A kitchen in Liu Sha will help suppress and minimise these types of problems. The Firemouth direction in a Liu Sha kitchen should ideally tap into a favourable direction such as Yan Nian 延年 (Longevity).

House Facing South (Sitting North)

Auspicious 吉 ☐
Inauspicious 凶 ☐

延年 *Yan Nian* Longevity	生氣 *Sheng Qi* Life Generating	禍害 *Huo Hai* Mishaps
伏位 *Fu Wei* Stability	震 **Zhen House**	絕命 *Jue Ming* Life Threatening
六煞 *Liu Sha* Six Killings	天醫 *Tian Yi* Heavenly Doctor	五鬼 *Wu Gui* Five Ghosts

SE — S — SW — E — W — NE — N — NW

Auspicious 吉 ☐
Inauspicious 凶 ▨

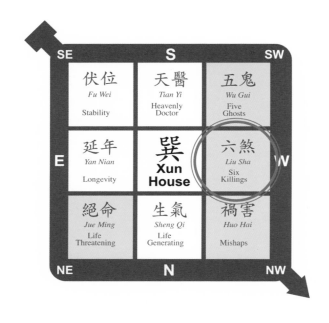

SE	**S**	**SW**
伏位 *Fu Wei* Stability	天醫 *Tian Yi* Heavenly Doctor	五鬼 *Wu Gui* Five Ghosts
延年 *Yan Nian* Longevity	巽 **Xun House**	六煞 *Liu Sha* Six Killings
絕命 *Jue Ming* Life Threatening	生氣 *Sheng Qi* Life Generating	禍害 *Huo Hai* Mishaps
NE	**N**	**NW**

(E on left, W on right)

Auspicious 吉 ☐
Inauspicious 凶 ☐

Auspicious 吉 ☐
Inauspicious 凶 ☐

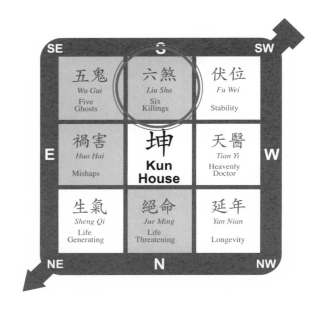

Auspicious 吉 ☐

Inauspicious 凶 ▨

House Facing Southeast (Sitting Northwest)

WEST GROUP
西宅

禍害 *Huo Hai* Mishaps	絕命 *Jue Ming* Life Threatening	延年 *Yan Nian* Longevity
五鬼 *Wu Gui* Five Ghosts	乾 **Qian House**	生氣 *Sheng Qi* Life Generating
天醫 *Tian Yi* Heavenly Doctor	六煞 *Liu Sha* Six Killings	伏位 *Fu Wei* Stability

Auspicious 吉 ☐

Inauspicious 凶 ▨

KITCHEN FORMS

153

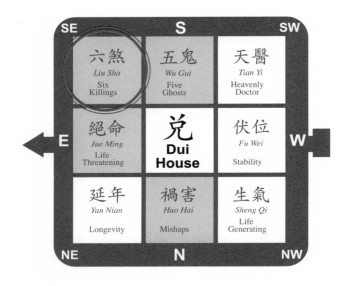

Auspicious 吉 ☐
Inauspicious 凶 ▨

絕命 *Jue Ming* Life Threatening	禍害 *Huo Hai* Mishaps	生氣 *Sheng Qi* Life Generating
六煞 *Liu Sha* Six Killings	艮 **Gen House**	延年 *Yan Nian* Longevity
伏位 *Fu Wei* Stability	五鬼 *Wu Gui* Five Ghosts	天醫 *Tian Yi* Heavenly Doctor

Auspicious 吉 ☐
Inauspicious 凶 ▨

Kitchen in Wu Gui 五鬼 (Five Ghost)

Wu Gui 五鬼 in the study of Eight Mansions, governs energies that result in life stress, niggling problems, gossip, backstabbing and gullible people who are easily conned or bamboozled into doing things (along with bad luck if you happen to enjoy playing mahjong, amongst other things). Obviously, a kitchen in Wu Gui helps you avoid some of these negative situations and certainly help reduces stress and work pressure. As always, the Firemouth must be orientated towards a favourable direction.

House Facing South (Sitting North)

生氣 *Sheng Qi* Life Generating	延年 *Yan Nian* Longevity	絕命 *Jue Ming* Life Threatening
天醫 *Tian Yi* Heavenly Doctor	坎 **Kan House**	禍害 *Huo Hai* Mishaps
五鬼 *Wu Gui* Five Ghosts	伏位 *Fu Wei* Stability	六煞 *Liu Sha* Six Killings

Auspicious 吉 ☐
Inauspicious 凶 ▨

House Facing West (Sitting East)

SE | **S** | **SW**

延年
Yan Nian
Longevity

生氣
Sheng Qi
Life Generating

禍害
Huo Hai
Mishaps

伏位
Fu Wei
Stability

震
Zhen House

絕命
Jue Ming
Life Threatening

六煞
Liu Sha
Six Killings

天醫
Tian Yi
Heavenly Doctor

五鬼
Wu Gui
Five Ghosts

E ← → **W**

NE | **N** | **NW**

Auspicious 吉 ☐
Inauspicious 凶 ▨

KITCHEN FORMS

157

SE	S	SW
伏位 *Fu Wei* Stability	天醫 *Tian Yi* Heavenly Doctor	五鬼 *Wu Gui* Five Ghosts
延年 *Yan Nian* Longevity	巽 **Xun House**	六煞 *Liu Sha* Six Killings
絕命 *Jue Ming* Life Threatening	生氣 *Sheng Qi* Life Generating	禍害 *Huo Hai* Mishaps
NE	N	NW

Auspicious 吉 ☐

Inauspicious 凶 ▨

SE 天醫 *Tian Yi* Heavenly Doctor	**S** 伏位 *Fu Wei* Stability	**SW** 六煞 *Liu Sha* Six Killings
E 生氣 *Sheng Qi* Life Generating	離 **Li House**	五鬼 *Wu Gui* Five Ghosts **W**
NE 禍害 *Huo Hai* Mishaps	**N** 延年 *Yan Nian* Longevity	**NW** 絕命 *Jue Ming* Life Threatening

Auspicious 吉 □

Inauspicious 凶 □

SE	S	SW
五鬼 *Wu Gui* Five Ghosts	六煞 *Liu Sha* Six Killings	伏位 *Fu Wei* Stability
禍害 *Huo Hai* Mishaps (E)	坤 **Kun House**	天醫 *Tian Yi* Heavenly Doctor (W)
生氣 *Sheng Qi* Life Generating	絕命 *Jue Ming* Life Threatening	延年 *Yan Nian* Longevity
NE	N	NW

Auspicious　吉　☐
Inauspicious　凶　▨

Auspicious 吉 ☐
Inauspicious 凶 ▨

Auspicious　吉 ☐
Inauspicious　凶 ▨

House Facing Southwest (Sitting Northeast)

WEST GROUP
西宅

Auspicious 吉 ☐

Inauspicious 凶 ▨

KITCHEN FORMS

163

Kitchen in Huo Hai 禍害 (Mishaps)

Huo Hai (禍害) relates to daily hassles in life and life endeavours. Huo Hai problems relate to difficulties with colleagues, problems at the workplace or with relationship, being ostracised socially and bypassed for promotions. Obviously a kitchen in Huo Hai helps keep these problems at a minimum and provides a smoother path in life as well as better health and good relationships. As always, the Firemouth must be orientated towards a favourable direction for a Huo Hai kitchen.

House Facing South (Sitting North)

Auspicious	吉	☐
Inauspicious	凶	▨

FENG SHUI FOR HOMEBUYERS - INTERIOR

164

SE	S	SW
延年 *Yan Nian* Longevity	生氣 *Sheng Qi* Life Generating	禍害 *Huo Hai* Mishaps
伏位 *Fu Wei* Stability	震 **Zhen House**	絕命 *Jue Ming* Life Threatening
六煞 *Liu Sha* Six Killings	天醫 *Tian Yi* Heavenly Doctor	五鬼 *Wu Gui* Five Ghosts
NE	N	NW

E ← → W

Auspicious 吉 ☐
Inauspicious 凶 ▨

Auspicious 吉 ☐
Inauspicious 凶 ▧

SE	S	SW
天醫 *Tian Yi* Heavenly Doctor	伏位 *Fu Wei* Stability	六煞 *Liu Sha* Six Killings
生氣 *Sheng Qi* Life Generating	離 **Li** **House**	五鬼 *Wu Gui* Five Ghosts
禍害 *Huo Hai* Mishaps	延年 *Yan Nian* Longevity	絕命 *Jue Ming* Life Threatening
NE	N	NW

E (left) — W (right)

Auspicious 吉 ☐
Inauspicious 凶 ▢

五鬼 *Wu Gui* Five Ghosts	六煞 *Liu Sha* Six Killings	伏位 *Fu Wei* Stability
禍害 *Huo Hai* Mishaps	坤 **Kun House**	天醫 *Tian Yi* Heavenly Doctor
生氣 *Sheng Qi* Life Generating	絕命 *Jue Ming* Life Threatening	延年 *Yan Nian* Longevity

Auspicious 吉 ☐

Inauspicious 凶 ▨

House Facing Southeast (Sitting Northwest)

WEST GROUP
西宅

Auspicious 吉 ☐
Inauspicious 凶 ▧

KITCHEN FORMS

169

Auspicious 吉 ☐

Inauspicious 凶 ▨

絕命 *Jue Ming* Life Threatening	禍害 *Huo Hai* Mishaps	生氣 *Sheng Qi* Life Generating
六煞 *Liu Sha* Six Killings	艮 **Gen House**	延年 *Yan Nian* Longevity
伏位 *Fu Wei* Stability	五鬼 *Wu Gui* Five Ghosts	天醫 *Tian Yi* Heavenly Doctor

Auspicious 吉 ☐
Inauspicious 凶 ▦

KITCHEN FORMS

171

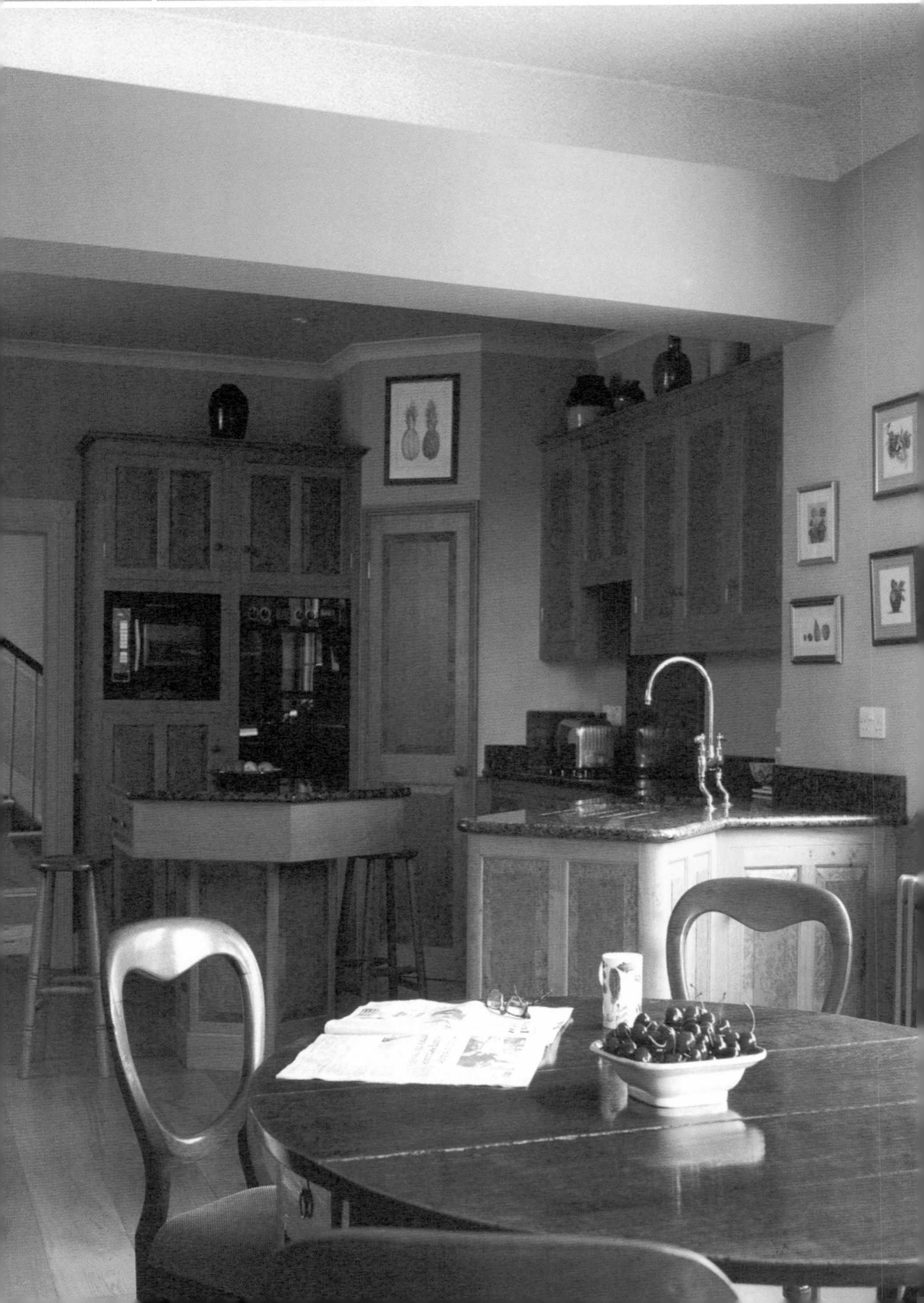

Chapter Four:
Bedroom Forms

The Bedroom is the last of the 3 most important factors of analysing internal Feng Shui, the other two being the Kitchen and the Main Door, which I have discussed in the preceding chapters.

What is the reason the bedroom is so important? Well, if you think about it, the bedroom represents the place that we spend 1/3 of our lives.

Sleeping and resting are important activities which impact on our health and vitality. Therefore the type of Qi that affects the bedroom is very important. Like the kitchen, bedrooms should be located in suitable sectors, based on the formulas in Eight Mansions (八宅), Xuan Kong Da Gua (玄空大卦) or Flying Stars (飛星) and according to what is suitable to the house, as dictated by the environmental conditions.

When looking at the bedrooms, the primary concern is not only to ensure Qi can enter the bedroom but we are also concerned with the positioning of the bed and location of the bedroom. Now, don't worry if you don't know anything about the formulas, which are used to position the bed and locate the bedroom in the right location. Observing the forms is equally, if not more important.

Violating any rules on the internal forms of the property will negate the advantage of locating the bedroom in a good sector and will aggravate the situation if the bedroom is located in a bad sector. Similarly, if the positioning of the bed is good, but if the bedroom has negative forms, you're still back at square one, with a bedroom that has negative Feng Shui Quotient (FSQ).

When screening the house and its rooms, like all the screening you've done for the macro environment and the micro environment, it is a question of priority. First, we want to make sure the bedroom itself has good forms or is not affected by negative forms. After that, we look into locating the bedroom in a good sector according to the formulas. The bed positioning (or facing direction), based on the headboard, comes later. If you get the forms right, you're already assured of a good Feng Shui Quotient (FSQ) for your bedroom. The positioning of the bed and location of the room are icing on the cake.

Shape of the bedroom

It is important that the basic shape of the room is squarish or rectangular. Remember in my previous book, *Feng Shui for Homebuyers – Exterior*, I said square or rectangular shapes represent Earth? The Earth element represents stability and thus, it is most suitable for activities like sleeping and working.

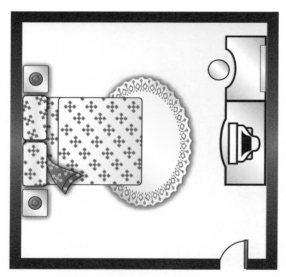

Square shape room

As far as possible, you should avoid rooms that are round, triangular, trapezium or odd shaped with sharp corners. Firstly, these rooms do not have a balanced flow of Qi, and thus they do not bode well for an activity like sleeping or resting. Secondly, if the Qi flow is not balanced, then during a year when there are negative visiting stars in that bedroom, the negative afflictions will become exacerbated, especially if the external forms are negative. By choosing a square room, you are to some degree, insulated from any negative Qi that may impact the room.

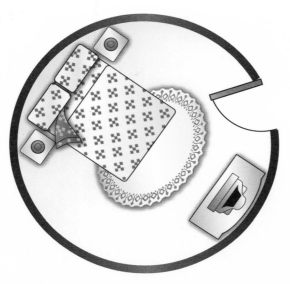

Round shape room: Metal Qi is too strong in a Round room

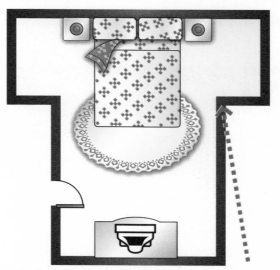

T shape room: Sha Qi generated by Sharp corner

*Locate the bedroom in the right sector,
before you worry about bed placement.*

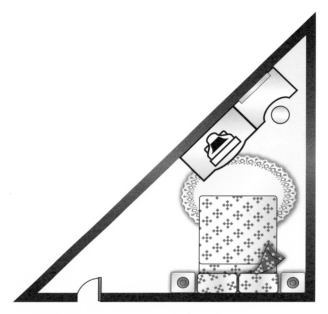

Triangular shape room: Qi is imbalanced in triangular rooms

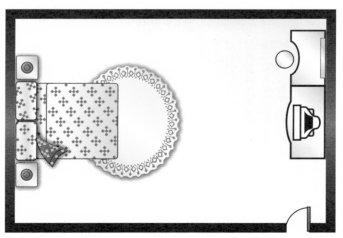

Rectangular shape room: Qi is balanced in a rectangular room

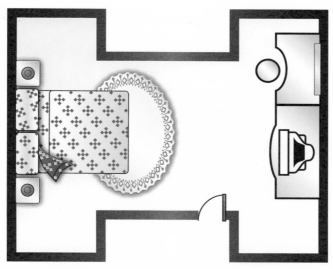

Dumbbell shape room: Qi is imbalanced

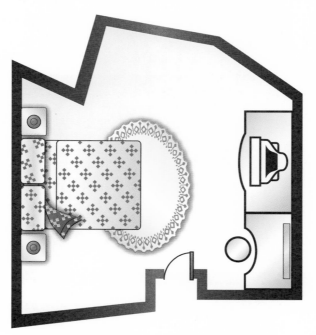

Irregular shape room: Qi is imbalanced

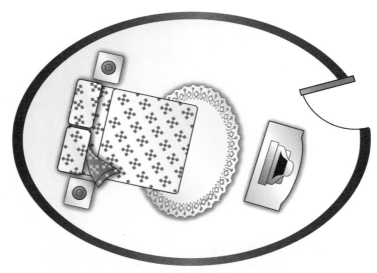

Oval shape room: It is not advisable to sleep in an oval shaped room.
It's better used as a meeting room!

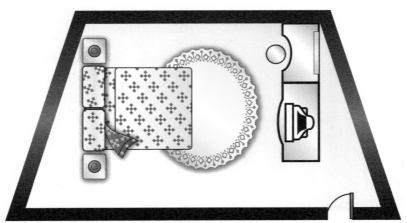

Trapezium shape room: Qi Flow is imbalanced.
Try to position the bed at the parallel walls for stability.

L-shaped rooms

Many people avoid L-shaped rooms but only because they think that such rooms are knife shape rooms, and thus the room cuts into your life. Here's the real explanation: the L-shaped room causes the Qi to be imbalanced and you instantly have a problem wherein certain sectors of the Ba Gua are missing. You also have a problem of in-built Sha Qi (煞氣) from the sharp corner the L creates. If you do find you have a L-shaped room, it is quite easy to rectify – square off the room with a walk-in wardrobe.

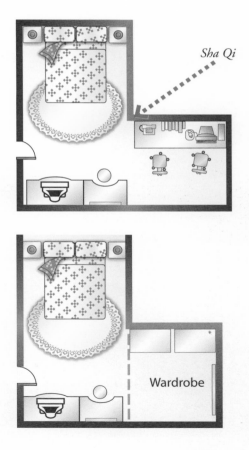

Sha Qi

Wardrobe

Sleep is a Yin activity and thus, the bed, in which we undertake the activity of sleep, should therefore be positioned against a Yin feature. Clearly, sleeping against a Yang feature will create an imbalance in sleep, resulting in a decline in performance and health problems for the person.

So what is Yin and what is Yang in a bedroom? A window, which is an open space, is Yang. The wall, which does not move, is Yin. Hence, always position the bed against the wall. When I say the bed should be positioned against the wall, I mean the headboard of the bed should be placed against a wall.

Bed against a solid wall - the bed is against a Yin element.

Bed against glass windows - the bed is against a Yang element.

Do not forsake this simple principle in the name of tapping
your favourable direction. Often, this causes the bed to be
positioned at an angle, with head against a corner. So while they
have achieved the favourable direction, they have also instantly
created Sha Qi that points directly at their head! Irrespective of
direction, putting your bed so that the headboard is at an angle
towards a corner exposes you to Sha Qi.

Sha Qi

Use some common sense – put the bed against a wall, even if it
is not facing your good direction. The stability of the wall will
ensure a good night's sleep. Obviously, it is ideal to position
the bed so that you sleep with your head pointing towards
your personal best directions but in Feng Shui, there are times
when discretion and indeed, some common sense is required.
Don't nit pick because you'll find sometimes, you end up with
something entirely worse altogether.

BEDROOM FORMS

Beams create suppressive Qi (壓迫). The beam will force the Qi entering the room downwards. This causes disrupted sleep and results in poor job performance and lots of problems and troubles for the person sleeping in the bed under the beam. In particular, health and work pressure problems will affect the person sleeping under the beam.

Beam

There is a saying in Chinese - Chuang Tou Zhao Jing, Shen Ti Duo Bing 床頭照鏡，身體多病 . The bed faces a mirror, the health has many illnesses. This is yet another one of those neat Chinese rhymes that has grown into a Feng Shui fact with a life of it's own. Here's the truth: in Feng Shui, there is no problem having a mirror in front of your bed, or any reflective surface. Psychologically, it may be a nuisance as this reflective surface will catch and reflect light, thus potentially disrupting sleep. So for this reason, you may not want to have your bed positioned this way. But in itself, the mirror is not causing any Feng Shui problem, be it a third party in the relationship or bad luck.

Bed with windows at the back.

This is a situation the windows are behind the headboard of the bed. Windows are Yang and thus because it is Yang Qi and the sleep is Yin, the situation is not balanced. Furthermore, wind from the windows will hit the head and the person is regarded as sleeping in a position without solid backing. Not a very good bed position but again, not a cause for major concern. Thick curtains, with the windows kept closed while you sleep, will solve the problem.

Avoid positioning the bed against the windows

There is a very strange paranoia about four poster beds and somehow, people think they are bad Feng Shui. They are not. Your bed design, the colour of your blanket or pillows, have no bearing on your Feng Shui. Remember, it is position and location that matter. If you like four poster beds, then sleep in one!

Feet pointing at room door

If your bed directly faces the bedroom door, with your feet pointing towards the room door, it is sometimes said that the person is sleeping in the 'coffin position'. Now, this business of 'coffin position' is really an old wives tale – you are not actually sleeping in a coffin after all. This position IS bad Feng Shui, but has nothing to do with coffins. Rather, this position means that the Qi entering the room through the door crashes into the bed, causing interrupted or bad sleep. The solution is quite simple – move the bed so that you are not sleeping, head or foot, in direct alignment with the bedroom door.

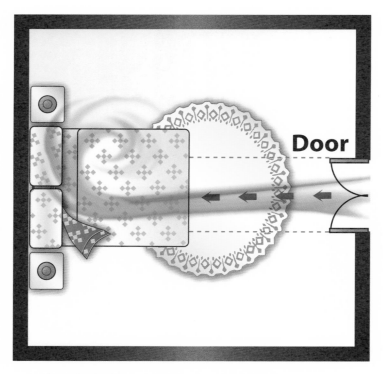

When the bed is positioned directly in front of the door, there is Sha Qi hitting the bed.

Avoid sleeping directly in front of the Bedroom door.

Feet pointing to Downstairs Main Door

In Malaysia, it is common for the Master Bedroom to be located at the front of the house, on top of the Main Door. There is a myth going around that sleeping with your feet facing the direction of the Main Door, is also a version of the 'coffin position'. This is not just a myth, but utter nonsense. The Main Door does not affect you when you are sleeping upstairs. You are only affected if your feet or head actually are located in front of a real door, such as the door of the bedroom.

Sleeping with your feet pointing in the same direction
of the Main Door is not a problem.

Generally, a bed should not be positioned in alignment with any door, be it the bedroom door or bathroom door. This is because Qi from the door crashes right into the bed. If you cannot move the bed to any other position, then cut off the Qi from the bathroom by placing a screen between the door and the bed. Make sure that the screen is the same height as the door.

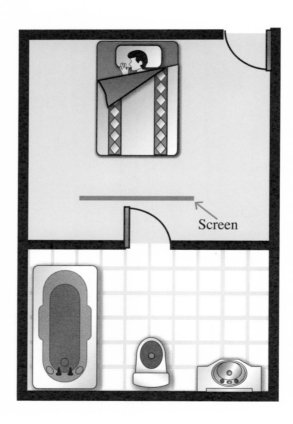

Screen

Place a screen between the bed and the bathroom door to circumvent the problem of the bed facing the bathroom door

Water beds

Water beds are not mentioned in the ancient texts but applying common sense, Water, being Yang, is not conducive to a Yin activity like sleeping. Also, I doubt it gives a good night's sleep. If you feel comfortable sleeping on one, fine but generally, I don't recommend it for long-term prosperity and harmony with your spouse.

Bedroom ceiling is slanted

A slanted ceiling causes the Qi in the room to be imbalanced as a result, sleep is disrupted and uneasy. Children who sleep in a room with a slanted ceiling are usually rebellious or restless. There are several possible solutions, one is to straighten out the ceiling. However, if this is not possible, then move the bed so that you sleep at the higher end of the ceiling, rather than the lower end.

Sometimes, a basement room is converted into a bedroom. Basically, the main consideration is whether or not there is enough Qi and light. If the room is really underground, with no natural light or it is stuffy and dank, indicating bad circulation of Qi, then it is not advisable to use this room as anything more than a storeroom or cellar. It is best not to use such room as a bedroom irrespective of direction or location. However, this does not apply when we are evaluating a commercial property such as a shop or mall, where it is obviously more spacious and with better Qi circulation.

Many people are concerned when their kitchen is below the bedroom, thinking that the fire in the kitchen is detrimental. This is a matter of small concern and is only relevant if the person sleeps directly above the stove. Mainly, mood is affected rather than anything else and people who sleep above the kitchen will probably just be a bit more moody, cranky or temperamental. The main consideration is also the ceiling height – if the height of the kitchen ceiling is substantial, then this is not a real problem.

Open Shelves in the Bedroom

Some people say that open shelves represent Sha Qi as they look like cutting blades. This is not true – you can have open shelves in your bedroom, located wherever is convenient for your books or items.

Some bedrooms have a pillar right in the middle of the room, sometimes to hold up a unique ceiling or perhaps due to renovation by the previous owner. This is known as a Pole in the Heart Formation and is not a good formation. Such a formation affects the circulation of Qi in the room and disturbs the central Tai Ji (太極) of the room. Another reason why such rooms are not good is irrespective of where the bed is located, there will be an internal Sha Qi pointing at the bed.

Bedroom Door opening to Spacious Area

This is a good formation as it means the bedroom door opens to a mini Bright Hall, where Qi can collect and circulate before entering the other rooms.

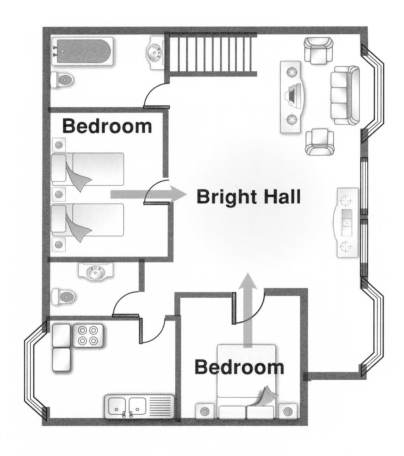

*An open space outside the Bedroom creates a mini-Bright Hall
- this is good for allowing Qi to collect and circulate.*

Bedroom door faces another bedroom door

Many people regard this as bad Feng Shui because the bedroom door faces another bedroom door. This is not a detrimental situation but is not favourable. Why? Because Qi should meander, and not flow in a straight line between rooms. The main thing to consider is the distance between the rooms. Obviously, if you have a landing or an open space or a good distance between the two doors, then it is fine.

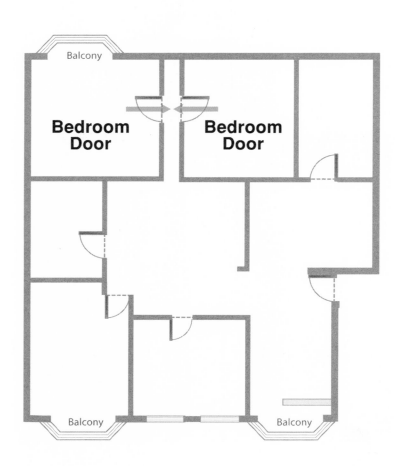

*Try to avoid having a bedroom door open directly into another
bedroom door with only a narrow space between the rooms.*

Bedroom Door faces Edge of Wall

The corner of the wall obviously creates Sha Qi pointing at the bedroom door. This clearly affects the quality of the room, irregardless of whether or not it is in a good sector or the bedroom door opens in a good direction. This type of room should probably not be used as a bedroom or you need to buy a cabinet to straighten out the corner.

This bedroom door is affected by Sha Qi from the sharp corner.

Bedroom location

Besides evaluating the forms, you may want to look into selecting rooms located in the positive sectors of the house, for optimal effect. For selection of bedroom locations, we use the House Gua method. So before you can determine if the bedrooms are located in a good or bad location, you need to first know the House Gua and determine the negative and favourable sectors.

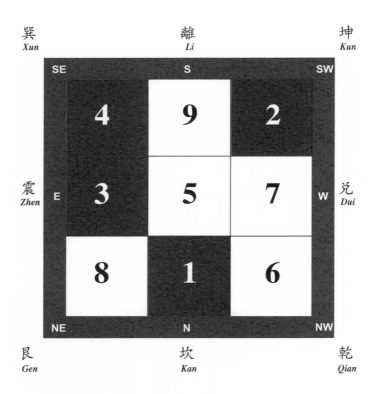

*You must first determine the House Gua of your house
in order to identify the rooms most suitable for bedrooms.*

Bedroom in Sheng Qi 生氣
(Life Generating)

Sheng Qi (生氣) is regarded as the Wealth sector in Eight Mansions Feng Shui. Qi is active here and brings about good prospects in career and business. It gives occupants good health, good performance at work and good recognition of opportunities at work. It is a good sector for a bedroom to be located in.

西宅
West Group Houses

House Facing Northeast (Sitting Southwest)

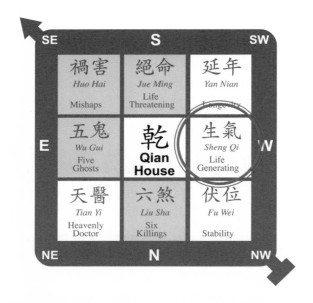

House Facing Southeast (Sitting Northwest)

Auspicious 吉 ☐
Inauspicious 凶 ▧

House Facing East (Sitting West)

Auspicious 吉 ☐
Inauspicious 凶 ▨

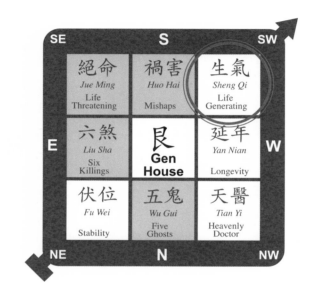

House Facing Southwest (Sitting Northeast)

Auspicious 吉 ☐
Inauspicious 凶 ▨

東宅
East Group Houses

House Facing South (Sitting North)

Auspicious 吉 ☐
Inauspicious 凶 ▨

House Facing West (Sitting East)

Auspicious 吉 □
Inauspicious 凶 ▨

House Facing Northwest (Sitting Southeast)

Auspicious 吉 ☐
Inauspicious 凶 ▨

House Facing North (Sitting South)

Auspicious 吉 □
Inauspicious 凶 ▨

Bedroom in Tian Yi 天醫
(Heavenly Doctor)

An excellent sector for those who would like good health and also enjoy 'noble people luck'. The Heavenly Doctor sector helps those who have poor health or who need rejuvenation of their health should sleep in a bedroom in the Tian Yi (天醫) sector if possible, especially elderly folks.

西宅
West Group Houses

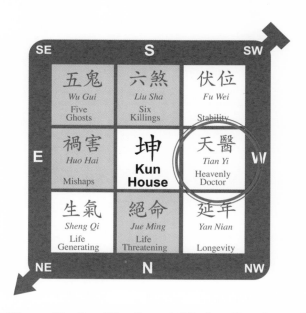

House Facing Northeast (Sitting Southwest)

Auspicious 吉 ☐
Inauspicious 凶 ▨

House Facing Southeast (Sitting Northwest)

Auspicious 吉 ☐
Inauspicious 凶 ▨

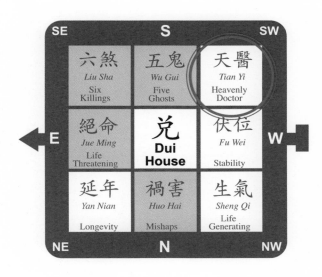

House Facing East (Sitting West)

Auspicious 吉 ☐
Inauspicious 凶 ▨

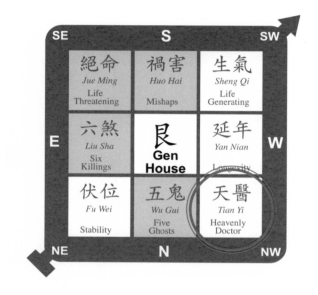

SE	S	SW
絕命 *Jue Ming* Life Threatening	禍害 *Huo Hai* Mishaps	生氣 *Sheng Qi* Life Generating
六煞 *Liu Sha* Six Killings	艮 **Gen House**	延年 *Yan Nian* Longevity
伏位 *Fu Wei* Stability	五鬼 *Wu Gui* Five Ghosts	天醫 *Tian Yi* Heavenly Doctor
NE	N	NW

(E on left, W on right)

House Facing Southwest (Sitting Northeast)

Auspicious 吉 ☐
Inauspicious 凶 ▨

東宅
East Group Houses

SE	S	SW
生氣 *Sheng Qi* Life Generating	延年 *Yan Nian* Longevity	絕命 *Jue Ming* Life Threatening
天醫 *Tian Yi* Heavenly Doctor	坎 **Kan House**	禍害 *Huo Hai* Mishaps
五鬼 *Wu Gui* Five Ghosts	伏位 *Fu Wei* Stability	六煞 *Liu Sha* Six Killings
NE	N	NW

E — W

House Facing South (Sitting North)

Auspicious 吉 ☐
Inauspicious 凶 ▨

House Facing West (Sitting East)

Auspicious 吉 ☐
Inauspicious 凶 ▨

SE	S	SW
伏位 *Fu Wei* Stability	天醫 *Tian Yi* Heavenly Doctor	五鬼 *Wu Gui* Five Ghosts
延年 *Yan Nian* Longevity	巽 **Xun House**	六煞 *Liu Sha* Six Killings
絕命 *Jue Ming* Life Threatening	生氣 *Sheng Qi* Life Generating	禍害 *Huo Hai* Mishaps

E / W on the sides, NE (bottom left), N (bottom center), NW (bottom right)

House Facing Northwest (Sitting Southeast)

Auspicious 吉 ☐
Inauspicious 凶 ▨

House Facing North (Sitting South)

Auspicious 吉 ☐
Inauspicious 凶 ▨

Bedroom in Yan Nian 延年 (Longevity)

Yan Nian (延年), translated verbatim means Longevity but does not relate to long life. Rather, it governs energies that help with fostering better relationships and ties. It is a sector that positively affects relationships and communications with friends, relatives or those seeking a Significant Other. This is a beneficial sector to locate a bedroom in general.

西宅
West Group Houses

House Facing Northeast (Sitting Southwest)

Auspicious 吉 ☐
Inauspicious 凶 ▨

House Facing Southeast (Sitting Northwest)

Auspicious 吉 ☐
Inauspicious 凶 ▨

House Facing East (Sitting West)

Auspicious 吉 ☐
Inauspicious 凶 ▨

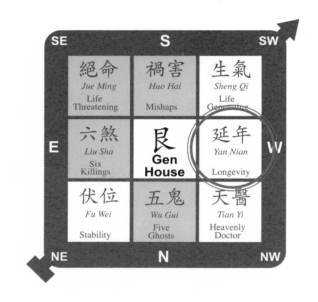

House Facing Southwest (Sitting Northeast)

Auspicious 吉 ☐
Inauspicious 凶 ▨

東宅
East Group Houses

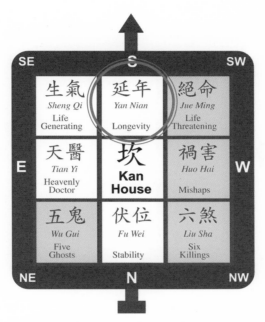

SE	S	SW
生氣 *Sheng Qi* Life Generating	延年 *Yan Nian* Longevity	絕命 *Jue Ming* Life Threatening
天醫 *Tian Yi* Heavenly Doctor	坎 **Kan House**	禍害 *Huo Hai* Mishaps
五鬼 *Wu Gui* Five Ghosts	伏位 *Fu Wei* Stability	六煞 *Liu Sha* Six Killings

E — W

NE — N — NW

House Facing South (Sitting North)

Auspicious 吉 ☐
Inauspicious 凶 ▨

House Facing West (Sitting East)

Auspicious 吉 ☐
Inauspicious 凶 ▨

House Facing Northwest (Sitting Southeast)

Auspicious 吉 ☐
Inauspicious 凶 ▨

House Facing North (Sitting South)

Auspicious 吉 ☐
Inauspicious 凶 ▢

Fu Wei (伏位) sector is a calming sector, best for those seeking personal cultivation or who have insomnia and wish to recover. It is good for meditation or study but is also ideal for a bedroom.

西宅
West Group Houses

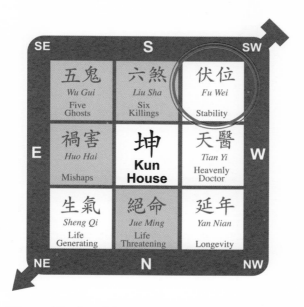

House Facing Northeast (Sitting Southwest)

Auspicious 吉 ☐
Inauspicious 凶 ▨

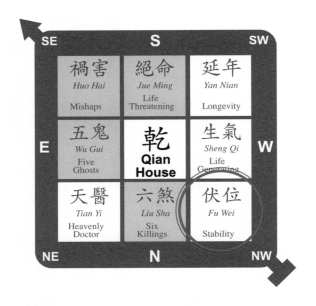

House Facing Southeast (Sitting Northwest)

Auspicious 吉 ☐
Inauspicious 凶 ▨

House Facing East (Sitting West)

Auspicious 吉 ☐
Inauspicious 凶 ☐

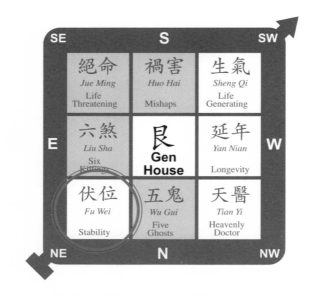

House Facing Southwest (Sitting Northeast)

Auspicious 吉 ☐
Inauspicious 凶 ▨

東宅
East Group Houses

House Facing South (Sitting North)

Auspicious 吉 ☐
Inauspicious 凶 ▨

House Facing West (Sitting East)

Auspicious 吉 ☐
Inauspicious 凶 ▨

House Facing Northwest (Sitting Southeast)

Auspicious 吉 ☐
Inauspicious 凶 ▩

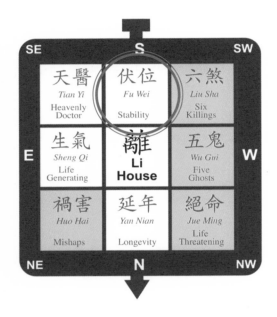

House Facing North (Sitting South)

Auspicious 吉 ☐
Inauspicious 凶 ▨

You can further refine the benefits of having a bedroom in a good sector by positioning your bed to tap to a positive personal direction. This is the way the House Gua and the Life Gua methods are used together, in tandem and in harmony, in a property.

Again, this is something that you can safely leave to your Feng Shui consultant to work out, especially if you can't be fussed with the formula-based assessment method. But for enthusiasts with a familiarity of Eight Mansions and who would like to go the one step further, I have included this section.

A house may have a bedroom with good forms, located in the right sector, but its architectural or interior design may not allow for a favourable bed location. This is something you may wish to consider or take into account when you are screening a property. For example, I have seen houses where out of 4 walls, 3 have glass windows. This essentially leaves only one wall for the bed which requires the occupant to sleep in an unfavourable direction. If you have a choice, you should consider if the house affords you the luxury of positioning your bed in a good direction.

Now, perfection is hard to come by. So don't be too hung up over not being able to have the perfect bedroom. Remember, it is a question of priorities. As long as the forms in the bedroom are positive, and the location is good, the fact that the bed is not in a favourable direction does not matter significantly. Remember, you don't need to get a perfect score, 2 out of 3 is pretty good.

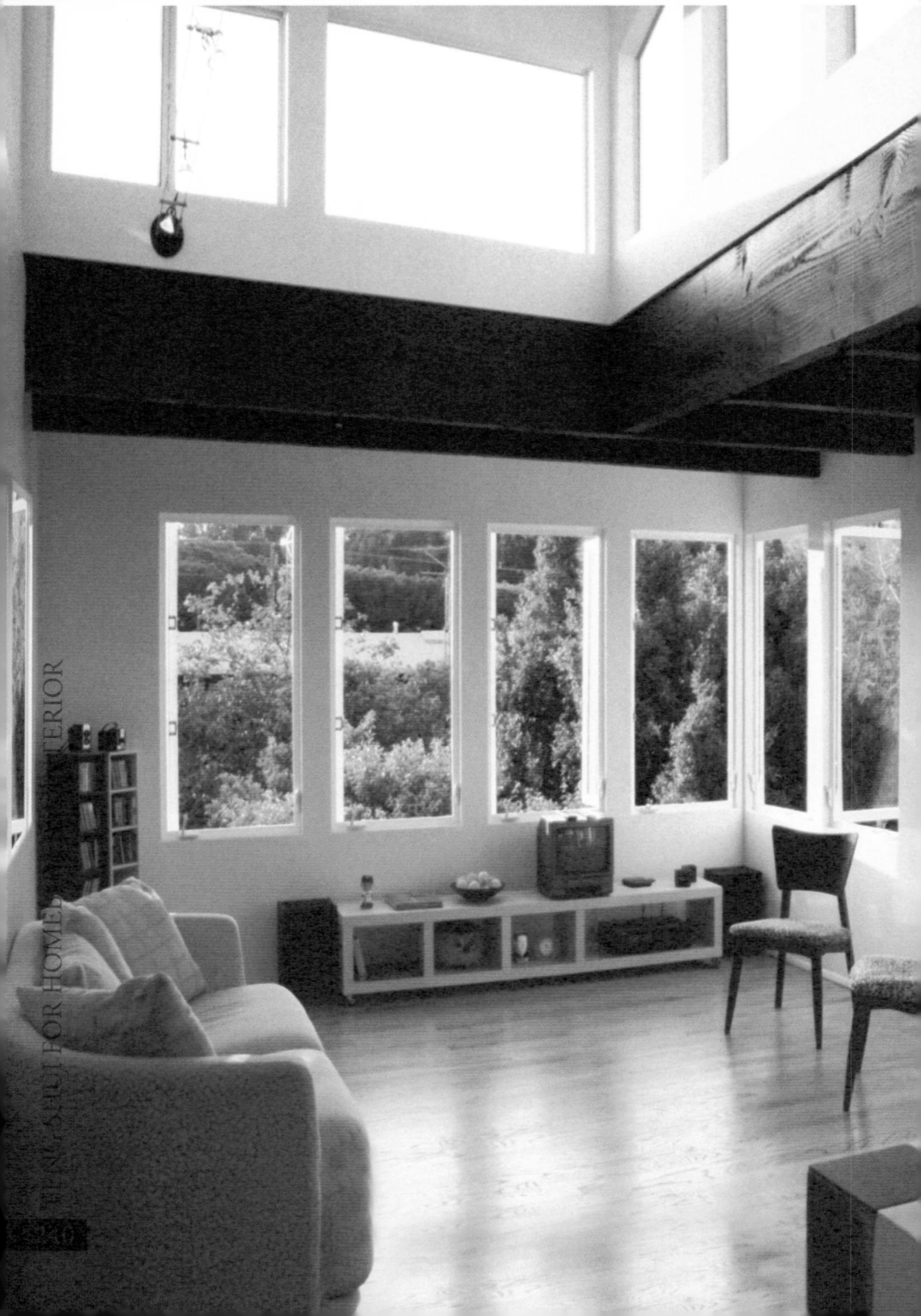

Chapter Five:
Common Internal Forms

In this chapter, I will discuss some of the common internal features found in houses and explain what circumstances these internal features are good or less favourable. These features should only come into your Feng Shui Vision when you have completed your evaluation of the external macro environment (the mountains and river formations discussed in *Feng Shui for HomeBuyers – Exterior*), and checked the Main Door, both looking in and looking out, which is extensively covered in Chapter 3.

Finally, do remember that not every unfavourable internal -*form you find represents a curable situation nor does every situation need curing. In some instances, you may well just be better off passing up on the property. Don't be afraid to do this. Remember, the goal is not to find a place you have to spend money fixing, but to find a place that already has good Feng Shui Quotient (FSQ) and which you can spend money improving!

Generally, most people live in double story homes these days. Accordingly, the staircase is one of the important internal features of a home a Feng Shui consultant will observe because it is through the staircase that Qi travels up to the second floor (and any subsequent floors) of the home. A carefully planned house is one where the staircase is located in an area where it can receive Qi and distribute it upstairs.

As the staircase is essentially a Secondary Qi mouth, it should be located in a sector, according to either Flying Stars or Eight Mansions, where it can benefit all the rooms upstairs.

There are some basic principles on forms that relate to staircases irrespective of their location which I will discuss here. But I hope you will note that these do not relate to the material you chose for your staircase, the colour, the banisters or for that matter, the flooring.

The Tai Ji 太極 of a property, also known as the Central Palace or the Heavenly Heart of the house, must, according to the tenets of Feng Shui, be kept stable and peaceful. This is to ensure there is a good flow of Qi into the house. This means the central palace must not be affected or disturbed in any way. A staircase in the middle of the property disrupts the flow of Qi in the property. Residents of a property with a staircase penetrating the central palace will not enjoy good health, and they will often have bad tempers, be constantly anxious and irritable.

To exert its maximum negative effect, the staircase has to be dead centre of the central palace. To check this, you will need to look at the architect's plan, which will contain the exact location. If the staircase is in the central palace but not dead centre, it is fine. However, to be on the safe side, avoid a house with such a feature.

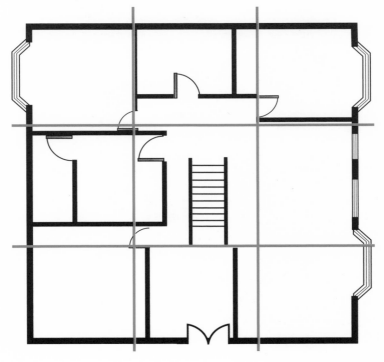

Spiral staircase

Spiral staircases are commonly regarded as bad in Feng Shui. I do not agree with this viewpoint. Staircases are just staircases in themselves, they are not a negative feature. How can they be a negative feature if you have a double story house? How then are people expected to get to the upstairs?

Spiral staircases are only negative when they are exceptionally narrow and located dead center in the central palace. In this case, you have corkscrew Qi penetrating the Heavenly Heart of the house. It doesn't take a lot of imagination to realise what happens - imagine sticking a corkscrew into your own heart! Heart attacks, stroke and sudden deaths will afflict the residents of the property with such a staircase in such a location.

Double Dragon Staircase

Staircases that curl up left and right are known as Double Dragon Staircases. This design is popular because they add grandeur and certain flair to a home. However, they are generally not suited to small or medium sized properties because they cause the Qi to split and go in two different directions.

Double Dragon Staircases that are located right in front of the Main Door create Qi imbalance because the Qi is flowing out too quickly. The people sleeping upstairs will usually experience relationship problems or separation. If you would like to have double staircases, it is best to split the staircase or modify the design so that it does not look like a collar. There is of course an exception to this rule but that only applies to very large buildings, such as hotels, wherein Double Dragon Staircases are permissible.

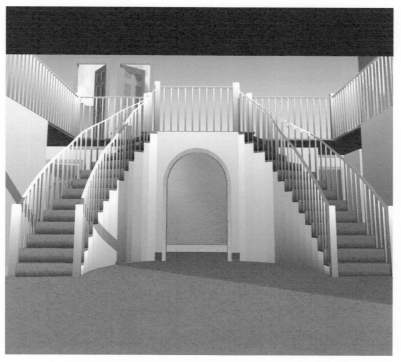

A staircase that runs directly above the Main Door is a negative form in the house but people often have the wrong idea why this is bad. Culturally, it is thought to be unfavourable because people are 'stepping' on you before you come into the house. But what is the real Feng Shui reason why it is bad?

The staircase is suppressing the Qi at the Main Door, forcing Qi out of the Main Door. Remember what I said in earlier chapters? We don't want to have any forms within the house or in proximity to the Main Door that repel or squeeze out Qi. A staircase on top of the Main Door exerts an effect similar to a beam above the Main Door. It also lowers the ceiling space at the door and cuts into the Internal Bright Hall.

Main Door

This is considered a beneficial staircase. It is better to have a staircase in the corner and not next to the Main Door.

As a general rule, staircases that have more landings are better because the Qi meanders and has a place to collect before moving to the next level. Staircases that are straight push up merciless Qi that gushes too strongly, especially if the stairs are steep.

Qi should meander through the property so in Feng Shui, staircases with landings are preferred over those without landings.

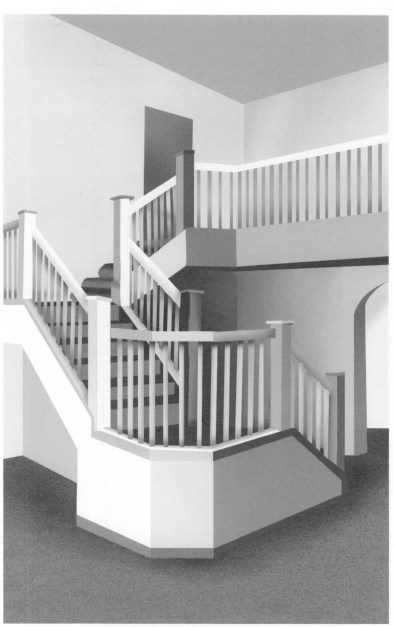

Staircase with landings.

Staircase leading down to a room

A staircase should not lead directly to any room unless the room is used as a storeroom. When a staircase, especially a steep staircase, leads up or leads down into a room, Qi is rushing in and hitting the door. Qi that enters the room or affects the room is volatile and not benevolent. Volatile Qi causes illness, health problems and relationship problems. Basement rooms usually have this problem. Always create a landing so that Qi collects and settles before entering the room.

*A room at the bottom of a staircase will usually
be affected by very volatile Qi.*

Staircase leading to master bedroom

It is essential that there is a landing before the staircase opens to the Master Bedroom. If there is a landing, then there is a small Bright Hall and Qi therefore has the opportunity to collect before it is gently sent up into the Master Bedroom. If the Master Bedroom door immediately opens to the staircase, then the property has a negative internal form called Pulling Nose Water (Qian Bi Shui 牽鼻水). Pulling Nose Water sucks out all the Qi from the room, not something that you want in your home. Therefore, if you find a property has a staircase that opens to the Master Bedroom, make sure it has a landing and you won't have a problem.

Master bedroom

These days, it's not uncommon to find houses with water features, such as a small pond or an aquarium, built into the interior of the house.

The placement of Water is an important aspect of a Feng Shui consultation and really, is something that should be left to the professional as incorrect placement could create serious problems for the occupants. Water substantially affects the flow of Qi in a property and is something that should always be given due consideration. Water in the right place encourages positive Qi flow. Water in the wrong place may create drastic outcomes or a violent flow of Qi.

This section deals with some of the common scenarios involving interior water features. For safety, it is best to avoid any property with internal water features or to only purchase the property after you have had the position of the water verified by a qualified Feng Shui consultant.

Pool cutting into house

This is a new modern/contemporary design that I have seen in quite a few houses. The pool is built, almost 'into' the house, so that the occupants can open a side door and hop straight into the pool.

The main consideration here is whether or not the pool touches the central palace of the house. If it cuts into the house substantially and touches the central palace, it is a problem and the sector the pool occupies will be affected.

What kind of problems will the occupants experience? It depends on the sector. For example, if the pool cuts into the West sector, then Dui Gua is affected. Dui Gua represents the youngest daughter but also indicates legal problems caused by things that are said, as Dui Gua also represents speech. If it is the South sector that is cut into, then heart problems, like a heart attack or blocked arteries, are likely.

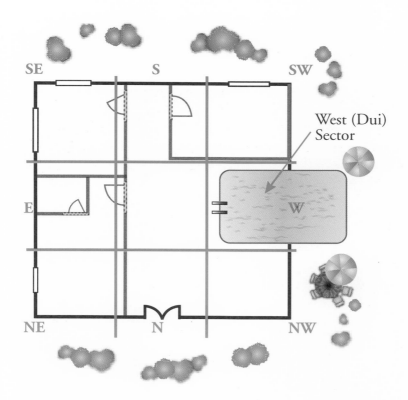

*This diagram shows a property with a swimming pool that cuts into
the house, creating a large body of water in the West sector.*

Pond in the center of the house

You want to avoid buying a house with a pond or body of water in the centre. The centre is the heart of the house and the central palace should always be Yin, and should not be Yang. It must be stable and quiet in the centre. Water is a form of excessive Yang Qi especially if it is a pond. It thus creates an active and moving centre. The flow of Qi in the property becomes disrupted and the occupants will usually experience poor health or in worst case scenarios - disastrous sudden outcomes. Exceptions to the rule do exist of course, but to err on the side of safety, avoid a house with such an internal form.

Swimming pool above the Main Door

In Classical Forms study, a swimming pool above the Main Door or the porch, is known as Lin Tou Shui (淋頭水) or Wetting the Head Water. It is an extremely detrimental formation and can cause significant loss of wealth, even bankruptcy. The key is to check the location of the door as long as the Main Door is not actually directly underneath the pool, it is fine. To be on the safe side, avoid a property with such a feature.

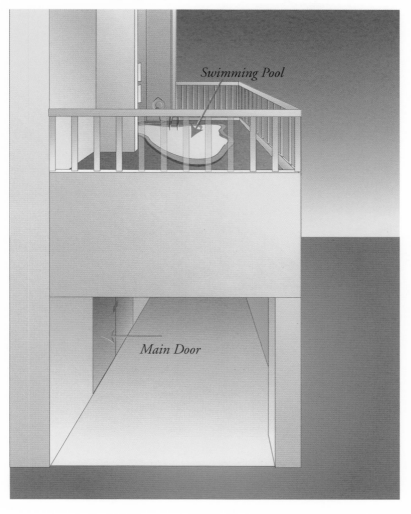

Swimming Pool

Main Door

Waterfall inside the house

Whether or not a waterfall inside the house is a negative feature, depends a lot on the sound it generates. Loud gushing or thunderous noise is definitely negative. However, if the waterfall creates a pleasant sounding, gently rippling or gurgling noise only, then it is fine. However, even then, you need to consider if it is located in a suitable sector for Water in the house.

Water Below Stairs

Some house owners build a pond underneath the staircase, for aesthetic or Feng Shui problems. This is a problem if the staircase is close to the center of the property because the water and the staircase both disturb the central Tai Ji (太極) of the property. We do not like to touch or disturb the central Tai Ji of the property. Accordingly, you should avoid such a property.

Aquariums

This is a popular 'interior Feng Shui' question. The Mailbag section of my book, **Stories and Lessons on Feng Shui**, lists a few of the typical questions I receive when it comes to matters related to aquariums. However, I will address one or two common concerns when it comes to aquariums and interior Feng Shui. Of course, it is rare to buy a house with a built in aquarium, but just in case, I will address that issue here.

Size of Aquarium

If your aquarium is purely for recreation or fish rearing purposes, then really, it's up to you what size you want it. But it is important to recognise that a substantial sized tank will invariably assert some Feng Shui effect. Accordingly, if you plan to have a fairly large aquarium (anything in excess of 5 feet in length), it is best to consult a Feng Shui master before selecting a location to place it.

This really has more to do with personal preference rather than Feng Shui. It is a misconception that certain types of Fish bring Wealth or are Wealth magnets. This is plainly untrue. In Feng Shui, Water is often used to collect and circulate Qi. Feng Shui consultants, being practical people, know that it would be strange to ask a client to put a bucket or container of water in a specific location.

So, to facilitate the goal of Qi collection, and to avoid an ugly eyesore, Feng Shui consultants tell their clients to put a fish tank or aquarium in the location. The client gets the benefit of the Water in the right location to help with Qi collection, and a nice eye-pleasing sight. Fish are usually added to help keep the water active – Water you will recall, is Yang in Feng Shui.

In essence, it is up to you what fish you put in and how many you put into the aquarium. What is more important is that the aquarium is located in the right sector or positioned appropriately.

Location of Aquarium

In Feng Shui, Water is used to collect and stimulate Qi and aquariums are often used to achieve this purpose, for aesthetic and practical reasons. I will not be delving into the Xuan Kong (玄空) or San He (三合) system of Water placement works here, as the goal of this book is to help you screen a house.

I have provided guidance on location of aquarium in the event some readers happen to be avid fish collectors or fish breeders and who will invariably have a fairly large aquarium in their home because of this hobby. I have also included this guidance in case you happen to chance upon a house which has a built in aquarium that cannot be removed for some reason.

In these situations, it is important to know if the house not only can accommodate your aquarium, but can accommodate it in a SAFE location, where the Water will not adversely affect the property and its Qi.

Up until 2043, the Southwest, East, North and Southeast are
safe sectors to locate your aquarium. If the Flying Stars of the
house and external Luan Tou (巒頭) forms are good, then this
aquarium may well even help bring favourable Qi and support
you in your endeavours, especially in financial matters.

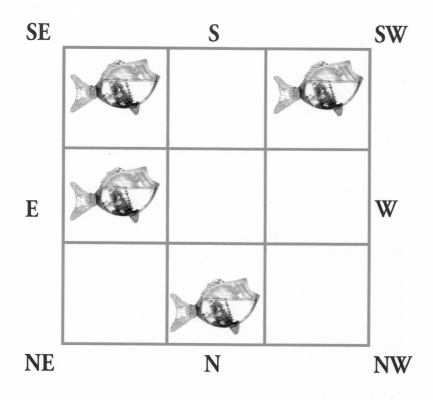

*Up until 2043, the Southwest, East, North and Southeast
are safe sectors to locate your aquarium.*

It is something that often concerns many people. It is one of the most common questions I get during any consult: where should the toilets be? Some clients seem to think that toilets are a highly negative aspect of any home and seem to even be willing to consider giving up the convenience of en-suite toilets, just to avoid having the "bad energies" in their room! Now, this is really taking things beyond the boundary of not just Feng Shui, but common sense.

Many people are under the (false) impression that toilets flush away wealth or that toilets are a negative feature in the house because they emit negative Qi. We live in modern times - toilets are clean and are generally hygienic so do not cause a problem of bad Qi. We are not talking about the toilets in rural China here! And anyway, just for the sake of argument, let's say the toilet was dirty and emitted a smell. Clean it and the problem goes away! Now, of course, this is not to say that the location of toilets is not significant in Feng Shui. It is a consideration, but only in the instances indicated overleaf.

Now, when I say the toilet is above the Main Door, I mean the actual toilet bowl itself (or a bathtub) is squarely above the Main Door. Just because the toilet room itself occupies the sector above the Main Door, does not mean the toilet bowl or bathtub are directly above the Main Door.

In the event the toilet bowl or a bathtub is squarely above the Main Door, then the house has a problem of Lin Tou Shui 淋頭水 or Wetting the Head Water Sha. This means there is an excess of Water Qi above the Main Door, creating a body of negative Qi surrounding the door area. The solution for this kind of problem is quite simple – either move the Main Door inwards, outwards or relocate the toilet bowl. Alternatively, don't use that particular toilet, then there's no problem. However, do note that if the ceiling at the Main Door area is high, this is not a problem.

Toilet above the kitchen

Sometimes, inadvertently in a property, there is a toilet above the kitchen. The excessive Water Qi above the toilet obviously affects the Fire element of the kitchen. But this is only really a cause for concern if the stove is located directly underneath the toilet bowl. For the sake of argument, let's say you do come across a house that actually has the stove directly under the toilet bowl (not just the toilet room). Just move the stove - a simple solution! By the way, you only need to be concerned about such a situation if the kitchen also has a low ceiling. If the ceiling is 15 feet and above, then the toilet above is not a problem.

This is not a problem unless you are sleeping directly underneath the toilet bowl. At the risk of sounding a bit indelicate, people often think sleeping in a bedroom underneath the toilet is bad because, you are, so to speak, subjected to faecal matter while you are asleep. This is not the reason why a toilet above the bedroom is bad. A toilet bowl above the bed, where the bedroom has a low ceiling (less than 12 feet), creates a problem of Wetting the Head Water Sha (Lin Tou Shui 淋頭水). The solution is simple enough – just move the bed!

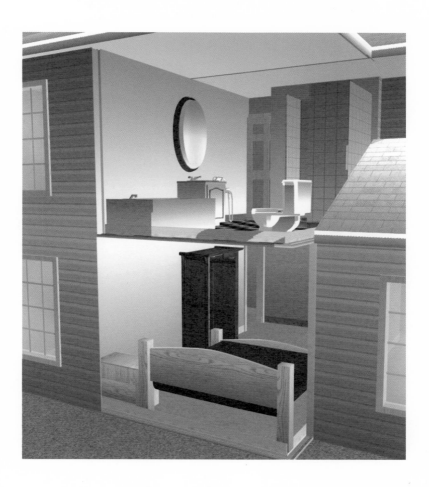

Room door opens to toilet door

This is quite a common feature in smaller homes. In this situation, all the Qi that enters the bedroom, immediately is deposited in the toilet, instead of circulating the room. This is not a good internal layout for a property so avoid buying a house with this problem. You may, if space permits, position some furniture in between the room door and the toilet door to fix this flow.

I have had a few clients who expressed concern because their bed headboard was against the wall that is next to the toilet or against a wall that is the toilet's wall. This is really not a problem – aside from perhaps some sleep disturbance caused by flushing noises at night, it is not an issue, Feng Shui or otherwise.

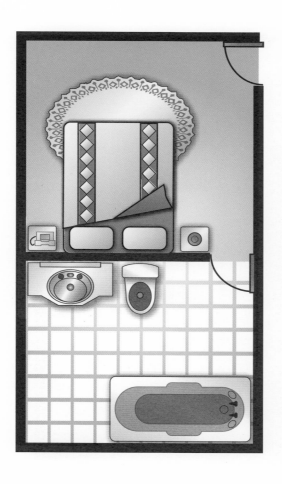

Toilet above dining room

This is really more a psychological issue rather than anything else. There is really no need to be concerned unless you actually have a problem with a leak in the toilet. In any case, from a Feng Shui point of view, you only really need to be concerned if the dining room is directly below the toilet bowl.

Some properties have a staircase that leads directly into the toilet. In this instance, the Qi ends up going into the toilet and being trapped in the toilet room, rather than circulating around the property. Generally such a formation is not favourable as we do not like to have Qi stagnant or trapped in one room.

Chapter Six:
What is not important in Interior Feng Shui

More often that not, I have met clients who are surprised that I have nothing to say about their interior design, no suggestions on colours for certain rooms, and don't seem to have any thoughts on their kitchen cabinets. It's the unfortunate truth that with the increased public interest in Feng Shui, comes increased superstition about Feng Shui.

Really, there is absolutely no reason to be fearful or paranoid. Remember, Feng Shui is practical. Its aim is to improve the quality of life of the occupants of a home. Not dictate their personal taste in décor or artwork. However, I thought it be pertinent to include a section in this book with some of the common questions I have received about items found inside a home and to debunk their Feng Shui value.

Colours and colour schemes

Curtains, cabinets, walls, tiles, carpets – the colour of these items are really personal choices, not Feng Shui decisions. Colours have more psychological impact on you than an actual Feng Shui effect. I always tell my clients, buy whatever colour that makes you feel comfortable or that you like. Now, this is not to say that colours have absolutely no Qi effect. They have a small 10% to a maximum of 15% (depending on how much of a colour is used) effect maybe on a room or on the occupants. But, this small positive effect is not going to be any good if you have to sit or sleep or work in a room that has a wall, carpet, tile, curtain or cabinet colour that you personally hate or do not like. For starters, you probably won't sit in that room so any 10% upside is instantly negated.

When you are screening a house, you should not be too concerned with the colour that the house is painted at present as it does not affect the property's Feng Shui. If you do not like the colour, just repaint the house to a colour you like. But the colour of the house in itself does not influence its Feng Shui.

Of course, if the ENTIRE house is painted Red for example or Black, then there is a problem because the property now has excessive Fire Qi (if it is Red) or Water element (if it is Black). But a patch of black or red or perhaps certain rooms being red or black or any other colour will not affect the Feng Shui of the property substantially.

Your carpet colour is matter of personal choice.

Feng Shui Dimensions

While many people are fastidious about how their home is constructed, some people go to extremes and require their home to have auspicious dimensions, according to what is measured by a Feng Shui ruler. There is no need to be this fastidious – Feng Shui dimensions are mainly for Yin Houses or tombs. For Yang Houses, this is not important so you can safely discard this concern.

Feng Shui measurements are not essential.

Tiles vs Wood floor

Again this is a matter of personal preference. Occasionally some clients take it a little bit far. For example, if their personal astrology chart or BaZi chart favours wood, they think everything in their house should be made of wood. It is certainly not practical in Malaysia, where humidity and termites make a 100% wood house a potentially problematic home. And in any case, what the property you live in is made of, contributes no impact to your Feng Shui. Remember, it's direction, location and the Qi map that counts, not what kind of material your house is made of.

The type of tiles in your home are not an important Feng Shui consideration .

Types of furniture

Feng Shui is about the Qi in the environment and the home, not about your personal taste. Your personal choice of furniture or decoration has no impact on the Feng Shui in your house. So collect whatever furniture you LIKE, and let your preference be the final arbitrator of what goes into your home, not Feng Shui.

Types of furniture are a matter of personal taste, not Feng Shui.

Size, design and colour of Main Door

The location and facing direction of the Main Door is the primary concern of the Feng Shui master. The door itself is not a big deal – so you can have sliding, grill, wooden, double door, single door or Japanese style doors if you want. The main consideration when it comes to the Main Door is the forms that are discussed in Chapter 2. The colour, size, design and material have no impact on the forms.

Main Door

I do have a lot of questions about toilets from clients, which I address extensively in my book, ***Stories and Lessons on Feng Shui.*** The main point to remember is that toilets, by the fact that we don't exactly spend a lot of time in there, do not have a substantial impact on the property or the residents. All this business of luck being flushed away, and toilets being Sha Qi are exaggerated New Age ideas. Generally, they are harmless and not really something to worry about.

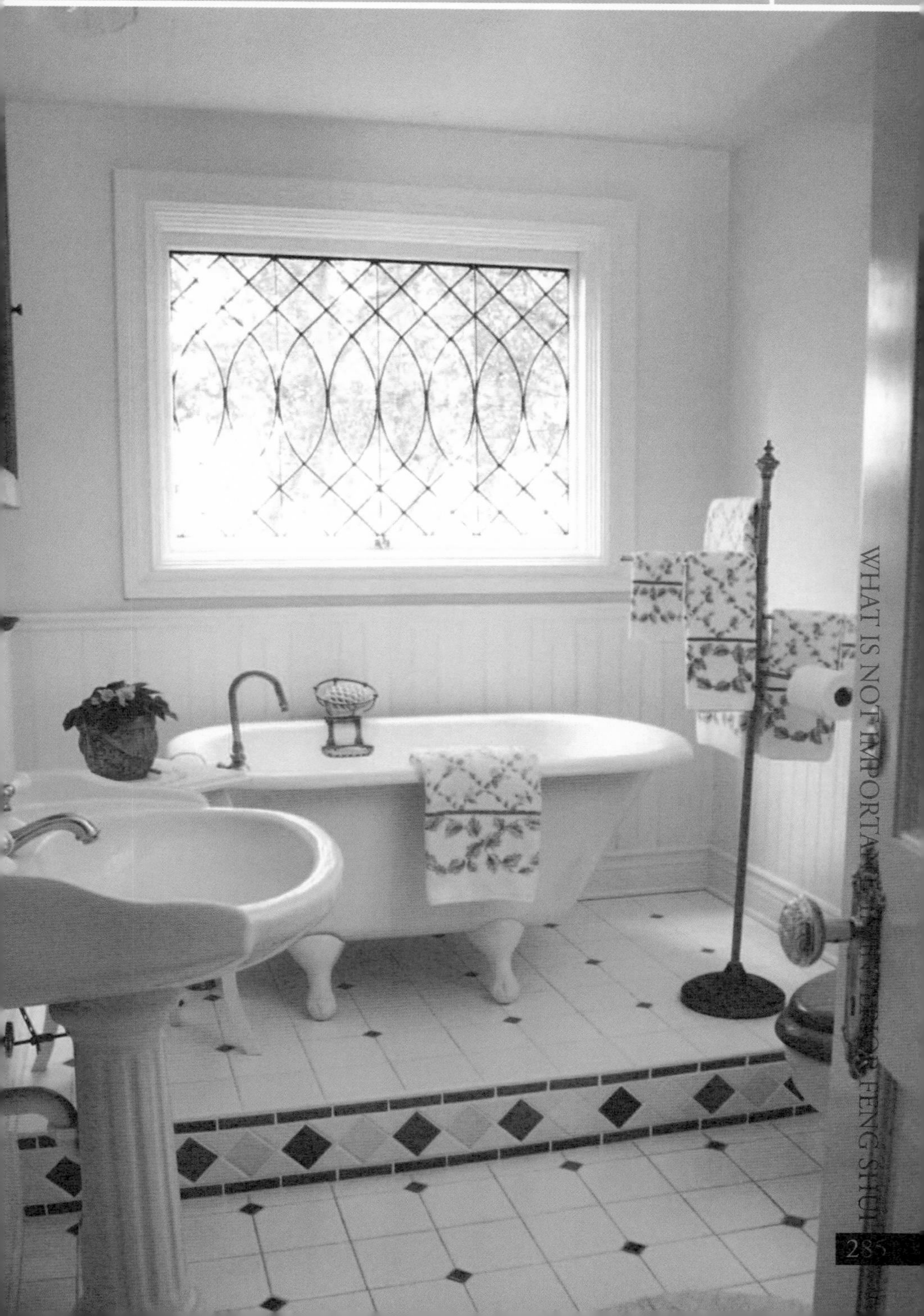

WHAT IS NOT IMPORTANT IN INTERIOR FENG SHUI

Paintings and Art

Auspicious paintings or calligraphy with inspirational wordings are fine for motivation or a psychological lift but they certainly do not result in any positive Qi for the room, no matter how auspicious the words are. There is nothing Feng Shui about paintings or auspicious calligraphy.

This applies to antiques and sculpture or any form of aesthetic decoration that you might want to consider for your house. You need to distinguish between the psychological impact of having say, ugly drawings or violent drawings or pictures or sculptures, and the Feng Shui of the house. The Feng Shui of your house is not affected by what items of decoration, be they modern art deco or ancient antiques, you put in various rooms.

Choose paintings that appeal to you.

Cactus In the House

The impression that anything SHARP is Sha Qi has resulted in some rather unfortunate misconceptions, including, the belief that you should never have cactus plants in your house!

The key is to always think of the big picture. Yes, sharp corners are Sha Qi but small pointy plants are not and they will certainly not send off Killing Qi in your direction simply because you have it on your desk at home. Remember, in Feng Shui, proportionality is important. A tiny little cactus cannot possibly generate any substantial negative Qi to harm you.

Water Pipes and Faucets

Some clients express a concern as to whether or not the pipes and faucets in their house are located in the right 'auspicious' locations. Yes, I am not joking! This is because some Feng Shui enthusiasts believe that pipes and faucets are regarded as Internal Water Mouths and thus must be located in the exact appropriate locations within the home. This concept is actually incorrect.

Water, or water inlets or outlets, have to be visible to the eye before the water can collect and harness Qi. Water also needs to be continuously running or visible in a certain volume in order to have any impact on Qi. Inside the pipes, water is clearly not visible. Accordingly, it is not important where your pipes run through or are located in the property.

Number of Steps on the Stairs

Some Feng Shui enthusiasts are of the view that the staircase must be a certain number of steps, and there is even a preference for odd or even numbers. The number of steps on the staircase inside your house is not relevant – this is just paranoia and superstition.

The number of steps you have leading up to your Main Door is also not of any significance. Some people feel that a house should have 5 steps to the Main Door, symbolising the Five Elements. This is a purely symbolic matter and has nothing to do with real Feng Shui. In fact, these 5 steps may actually be detrimental as, if the Main Door is too high from the ground level, it becomes very difficult for the house to receive Qi.

Double Leaf Door vs Single Leaf Door

Contrary to what you hear, it is not necessary to have an 'auspicious' door, which is what some people equate with double leaf doors. If you want an auspicious door, then make sure it is in the right location within the house and facing a good direction.

A bigger and wider door is of course better because more Qi can enter but that doesn't mean you need a giant castle-like door. It's more important to always make sure the door is in the right location, than its size and appearance.

Shoe Racks

Some people think that shoe racks near the Main Door is a bad sign – the Chinese say – Hai Hai 唉唉 (the word for shoe in Chinese) – sounds like the person is very sad, hence shoes should not be seen near the door. This is superstition, not Feng Shui.

Courtyards

There is a misconception out there that courtyards in houses are bad because they are akin to a hole in the centre of the house, causing Qi to leak out. In actual fact, courtyard are not considered bad Feng Shui – on the contrary, courtyards function as a place where Qi can circulate, enabling the Qi of Heaven and Earth to connect. When properly incorporated into the design of a property, a courtyard functions like a Heaven Well or Tian Jing 天井, enabling Qi to circulate from top to bottom, in and around the property.

Courtyards help collect and circulate Qi in a house

Ceilings

Clients are often concerned with the kind of ceilings that they can have in a home. Briefly, the guiding consideration when it comes to the ceiling is that it be of a simple design, with no excessive beams crossing the ceiling. Most of the time, however, it is not a major concern when it comes to the Feng Shui of a house.

Previous Owner Syndrome

Many people often refuse to buy a house if they find out some-one has died in it. Real estate agents no doubt are familiar with this problem. Most of the time, it may not be a Feng Shui issue but a psychological consideration.

If you think logically about it, there are very few houses out there (unless they have recently been constructed) which can claim no one has ever died in the premises.

Treat the Feng Shui aspect of the house, and the spiritual is-sues of the house separately. If there is nothing wrong with the house, but perhaps you feel a little uncomfortable with the fact that someone had died in the house, then perhaps a spiritual cleansing is all it needs.

Of course, it is logical not to buy a house that was formerly a funeral parlour since the Qi of the house would be too Yin but normally, the fact that a previous occupant or resident died in the property does not necessarily mean the property has bad Feng Shui.

Number of Rooms

Some clients believe that they need to have odd-numbered rooms because the Chinese word for 'even' is 'Shuang' 雙, which sounds like 'to hurt'. This is again, superstition and old-wives tales at work. The number of rooms is not an issue you should be concerned with as far as the Feng Shui of the property is concerned.

The number of rooms in the house are not a Feng Shui consideration.

295

Number of Doors in the House

The number of doors the property has, is not something to be alarmed about or concerned about. Some people have the idea that if a property has two Main Doors, there are two Qi mouths and so this becomes a problem. The number of doors is never the consideration – what is more important is where these doors are located and the direction the doors face. For example, if you have a typical Victorian style house, where the front door and back door are aligned in a straight line, this is obviously not good but it has nothing to do with the fact that there are two doors. It is more to do with the positioning of the doors.

In fact, many modern houses are designed with more than one door – a simple single door and an extra sliding glass door. This is usually done to facilitate entertaining and parties in the house. The main thing to remember is that having more than one door is not a big deal, as long as those doors are not in use simultaneously or open all the time at the same time. If the house has more than one Main Door and those doors are constantly in use or always open, then Qi will be confused. As long as only one door is used to enter and exit the house at any one time, it is not an issue. What is more important is to look at where the door is located, the direction it faces and whether it is affected by any negative forms.

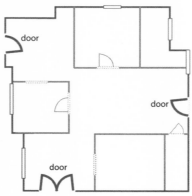

The Qi your property receives is determined by the Landform in the external environment.

Chapter Seven: Screening the Interior Forms

You should now be familiar with the concept of internal forms and the techniques for observing the interior forms of a property by this point. So, in this chapter, I'm going to show you how you undertake a systematic evaluation of a home, based on the information in the preceding chapters.

As I have emphasised throughout this book, the external forms in the macro environment ideally should be checked before the internal forms that are found within the home are examined. You should always ascertain if the property that you are considering is in fact, in an area that receives Qi and is able to collect Qi, before you look at the distribution of the Qi inside the house.

The checklist for evaluating the external forms is explained in the final chapter of ***Feng Shui for Homebuyers - Exterior***. But just to quickly recap the process: you need to identify the location of rivers and mountains in the vicinity of the property, mark these on a map, and obtain the Facing direction of your property, in order to demarcate the property into the 8 Directions. You then mark out any positive and negative forms that you have observed in the macro environment onto your plan of the property, to determine if any of these forms have an adverse impact, based on the Trigrams.

However, I also recognise that some of you may have bought this book after purchasing your property or are using it to evaluate a property you already own or already live in. In that case, you must recognise that you are restricted to evaluating the forms found within the interior of the property alone, although you still need to check for external forms because they may impact on your Main Door. Of course, you should never let what you cannot do limit what you can do so if you are restricted to merely evaluating interior forms, then aspire to have a home with as many positive interior forms as possible, and minimal negative forms.

To help you undertake the evaluation of Interior Feng Shui in a systematic way, I have devised a simple walk-through checklist for you to make use of. Now, this walk-through checklist bears some similarity to what a Feng Shui consultant will do when they undertake an audit of your house but bear in mind that your primary aim, as far as possible, is to screen the property, using this checklist. Evaluating the Feng Shui of a property using Landform Feng Shui is mainly about observation so after you have done some of the basic preparation work on your house plan, its time to turn on your Feng Shui Vision and start checking out the forms.

Step #1: Obtain an architect's plan or drawing of the house

A proper professionally drawn up map is essential when evaluating the interior Feng Shui. Don't rely on a map you have drawn yourself as your measurements may not be precise and your proportions may not be correct either. If you have to, pay an architect to undertake a drawing for you to scale.

Once you have a copy of the architect's drawing of the house, you can proceed to obtain the Facing Direction of the house. You will need this to demarcate the interior of the property into the 9 Palaces. The method for obtaining the Facing Direction of the House is explained in Chapter 1. Once you have obtained the Facing Direction of the House, demarcate the interior of the property according to the 9 Palace Grids, as explained in Chapter 1 using the 9 Palace stencil provided at the back of this book.

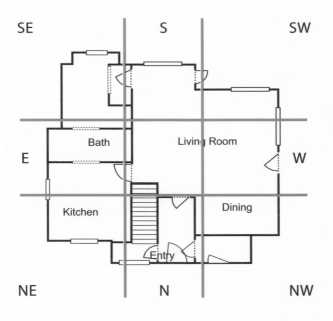

Step #3: Mark out the location
of the Main Door

Mark out the location of your Main Door, if this is not already marked out on your house plan. You may also want to mark out the existing location of the bedroom and kitchen. This will enable you to know what sector your Main Door, Kitchen and Bedrooms are located in, should you want to make use of formula-based assessment methods like Ba Zhai or Flying Stars.

*Main
Door*

Check to make sure that there are no sharp corners, pylons, roof corners, alleys, Crack in the Sky Sha or lamp posts or any of the negative features described in Chapter 2 visible from the Main Door. If there are negative features visible from the Main Door, make note of them and then check them against the Trigrams to see if they affect anyone in your family.

If you have ascertained that there are no negative forms affecting the Main Door, check to see if there are any positive forms, such as a spacious Bright Hall in front of the Main Door or a Table Mountain perhaps. You should also at this point, observe if there are any bodies of Water visible from the Main Door. Remember, you don't have to crane your neck or peer out at your neighbours. Just stand at the Main Door and look straight out.

Step #5: Stand at the Main Door and look in

Assuming your Main Door is not externally affected by any negative forms in the immediate proximity of the property, it's time to take a look inside. Stand at the Main Door, looking into the property and take a good look around. Are there any sharp corners pointing at the door from inside the house? Do you see any negative interior forms within a six foot range of the Main Door like a staircase or perhaps a beam pressing down on the Main Door? Take the time to also determine if there are any positive features, such as a spacious internal Bright Hall.

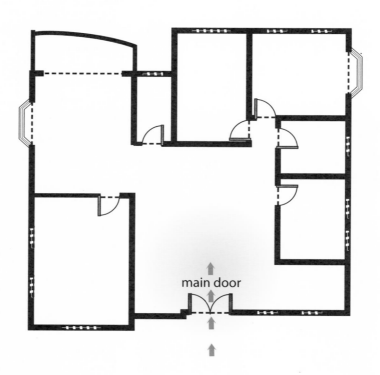

main door

Remember, the Main Door is the main Qi mouth of the house so we want to make sure it is not affected by negative forms. Assuming the Main Door is not negatively affected, then you can take the further step of checking the Direction of the Main Door against a formula-based assessment of the home. Ideally, you want the Main Door to face a good direction or be located in a good sector.

Step #7: Check the Kitchen and Bedrooms

Assuming your Main Door is not affected by any negative forms, then it's time to pay a visit to the kitchen and bedrooms. Ascertain that the kitchen and bedrooms are not affected by any of the negative forms outlined in Chapter 3 and 4 respectively. Of course, you may well have some flexibility with this because some houses may afford you the luxury of being able to determine which room to use as a kitchen and as a bedroom. But it is wise to check the forms in all the rooms anyway, in the event you want some flexibility with your design ideas.

Once you have checked the internal forms for the bedroom and kitchen and are satisfied that there are no negative forms or minor negative forms that can easily be rectifiable, you can go the extra step and check the location of the rooms against a formula-based assessment of the property.

Kitchen

Bedroom

Interior Water is something that you should be careful about as Water inside the house must be correctly placed in the right sectors or it can cause difficulties. If you do observe any large bodies of water (such as a pond or a built in aquarium) in any of the rooms, it is best to make note of which sector it is located in and have the property double-checked by a Feng Shui practitioner before you purchase.

Interior water features should be located at sectors conducive for water placement.

Finding the right home, with a good Feng Shui Quotient (FSQ) is not an easy matter. Often, people are tempted to do one of two things: try to find a perfect place (a very difficult task, especially if you are restricted by your budget) or get frightened into indecision.

To this, allow me to offer some advice on how to deal with this situation: prioritisation and patience. Unless you have the financial means to custom-design your home from the ground up, you should be prepared for the fact that any house you find or look at will probably have a Feng Shui wart or two. The trick would seem to be to determine if the flaw is minor or major, and whether or not it can be rectified through renovation or perhaps, changing the location of the Main Door for example.

However, this can be quite difficult for the lay person to judge, especially if you do not have a contractor at hand to answer your renovation questions and a Feng Shui consultant to confirm your renovation plans. So to err on the side of safety, you should as far as possible, aim to have a house with a good Main Door. If you have to sacrifice something else, then let it be. Keep your priority the Main Door.

But at the same time, you should also be prepared to say no if a house has major flaws when it comes to the Internal Forms. A house with a good Main Door but entirely unusable rooms due to negative forms, is a zero sum gain. Do not delude or kid yourself that the problem can be fixed or perhaps if you spend enough money on an expensive Feng Shui consultation, the problem can be solved. Remember, we don't want to have a problem in the first place. Don't just buy a house based on your favourable direction. The FORMS must first be evaluated. Direction is secondary.

*Forms must always be considered, before we look
at the formula-based assessment.*

Sometimes, it is a question of timing. If a person is going through good Heaven Luck (based on their Astrology chart) at that time, the chances of finding a good house or the right house, are better than someone looking for a house when they are down and out. So, if you find you keep chancing upon houses with certain flaws or nothing good seems to come along, it may well be wise to take a hint and postpone your search by a few months.

Do not be disheartened – the right home is out there for you and with a little bit of legwork, effort and patience, you should be able to find it.

Happy House Hunting!

9 Palaces Stencil

9 Palaces Stencil

About Joey Yap

Joey Yap is the founder and Master Trainer of the Mastery Academy of Chinese Metaphysics, a global organisation devoted to the worldwide teaching of Feng Shui, BaZi, Mian Xiang and other Chinese Metaphysics subjects. Joey is also the CEO of Yap Global Consulting, a Feng Shui and Chinese Astrology consulting firm offering audit and consultation services to corporations and individuals all over the world.

Joey received his formal education in Malaysia and Australia. He has combined the best of Eastern learning and Western education systems in the teaching methodology practiced at the Academy. Students of the Mastery Academy study traditional syllabuses of Chinese Metaphysics but through Western-style modular programs that are structured and systematic, enabling individuals to easily and quickly learn, grasp and master complex Chinese Metaphysics subjects like Feng Shui and BaZi. These unique structured learning systems are also utilized by Mastery Academy instructors all over the world to teach BaZi and Feng Shui.

The Mastery Academy is also the first international educational organisation to fully utilize the benefits of the Internet to promote continuous education, encourage peer-to-peer learning, enable mentoring and distance learning. Students interact with each other live, and continue to learn and improve their knowledge.

Despite his busy schedule, Joey continues to write for the Mastery Journal, a monthly eZine on Feng Shui and Astrology devoted for world-wide readers and the production of the world's first bilingual "Ten Thousand Year Calendar". He is also the best selling author of "Stories and Lessons on Feng Shui", "Mian Xiang- Discover Face Reading", "Tong Shu Diary" and "BaZi - The Destiny Code". Besides being a regular guest of various radio and TV talk shows, Joey is also a regular columnist for a national newspaper and various magazines in Malaysia, as well as being the host of "*Discover Feng Shui with Joey Yap*" on national 8TV Channel, a popular program which focused on education in Feng Shui and Chinese Metaphysics studies.

Author's personal website: www.joeyyap.com
Academy website: www.masteryacademy.com I www.masteryjournal.com

EDUCATION
The Mastery Academy of Chinese Metaphysics: the first choice for practitioners and aspiring students of the art and science of Chinese Classical Feng Shui and Astrology.

For thousands of years, Eastern knowledge has been passed from one generation to another through the system of discipleship. A venerated Master would accept suitable individuals at a young age as his disciples, and informally through the years, pass on his knowledge and skills to them. His disciples in turn, would take on their own disciples, as a means to perpetuate knowledge or skills.

This system served the purpose of restricting the transfer of knowledge to only worthy honourable individuals and ensuring that outsiders or Westerners would not have access to thousands of years of Eastern knowledge, learning and research.

However, the disciple system has also resulted in Chinese Metaphysics and Classical Studies lacking systematic teaching methods. Knowledge garnered over the years has not been accumulated in a concise, systematic manner, but scattered amongst practitioners, each practicing his/her knowledge, art and science, in isolation.

The disciple system, out of place in today's modern world, endangers the advancement of these classical fields that continue to have great relevance and application today.

At the Mastery Academy of Chinese Metaphysics, our Mission is to bring Eastern Classical knowledge in the fields of metaphysics, Feng Shui and Astrology sciences and the arts to the world. These Classical teachings and knowledge, previously shrouded in secrecy and passed on only through the discipleship system, are adapted into structured learning, which can easily be understood, learnt and mastered. Through modern learning methods, these renowned ancient arts, sciences and practices can be perpetuated while facilitating more extensive application and understanding of these classical subjects.

The Mastery Academy espouses an educational philosophy that draws from the best of the East and West . It is the world's premier educational institution for the study of Chinese Metaphysics Studies offering a wide range and variety of courses, ensuring that students have the opportunity to pursue their preferred field of study and enabling existing practitioners and professionals to gain cross-disciplinary knowledge that complements their current field of practice.

Courses at the Mastery Academy have been carefully designed to ensure a comprehensive yet compact syllabus. The modular nature of the courses enables students to immediately begin to put their knowledge into practice while pursuing continued study of their field and complimentary fields. Students thus have the benefit of developing and gaining practical experience in tandem with the expansion and advancement of their theoretical knowledge.

Students can also choose from a variety of study options, from a distance learning program, the Homestudy Series, that enables study at one's own pace or intensive foundation courses and compact lecture-based courses, held in various cities around the world by Joey Yap or our licensed instructors. The Mastery Academy's faculty and make-up is international in nature, thus ensuring that prospective students can attend courses at destinations nearest to their country of origin or with a licensed Mastery Academy instructor in their home country.

The Mastery Academy provides 24x7 support to students through its Online Community, with a variety of tools, documents, forums and e-learning materials to help students stay at the forefront of research in their fields and gain invaluable assistance from peers and mentoring from their instructors.

TM

MASTERY ACADEMY
OF CHINESE METAPHYSICS

www.masteryacademy.com

19-3, The Boulevard, Mid Valley City,
59200 Kuala Lumpur, Malaysia.
Tel: +603-2284 8080, +603-2284 8318
Fax: +603-2284 1218
Email: info@masteryacademy.com
Website: www.masteryacademy.com

Represented In:
Australia, Austria, Brazil, Canada, China, Cyprus, France, Germany, Greece, Hungary, India, Japan, Indonesia, Italy, Malaysia, Mexico, Netherlands, New Zealand, Philippines, Russian Federation, Poland, Singapore, South Africa, Switzerland, Turkey, U.S.A., Ukraine, United Kingdom

Mastery Academy around the world

Canada

United States

Mexico

Brazil

United Kingdom
Switzerland
Netherlands
France
Austria
Poland
Germany
Italy
Cyprus
Greece
Hungary

Russian
Federation

Ukraine

Turkey

Japan

China

India

South Africa

Philippines
Kuala Lumpur
Malaysia
Indonesia
Singapore

Australia

New Zealand

Feng Shui for Homebuyers Series

Feng Shui For Homebuyers (Exterior)

Best selling author and international Feng Shui consultant, Joey Yap will guide you on the various important features in your external environment that have a bearing on the Feng Shui of your home. A book that will benefit homeowners, those looking to build their own home or even investors who are looking to apply Feng Shui to their homes, this book provides valuable information from the classical Feng Shui theories and applications.

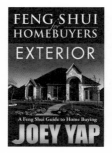

This book will assist you in screening and eliminating unsuitable options with negative FSQ (Feng Shui Quotient) should you acquire your own land or if you are purchasing a newly built home. This book will also help you in determining which plot of land to select and which are best avoided when purchasing an empty parcel of land.

Feng Shui for Homebuyers (Interior)

A book every homeowner or potential house buyer should have. The Feng Shui for Homebuyers (Interior) is an informative reference book and invaluable guide written by best selling author and international Feng Shui consultant, Joey Yap.

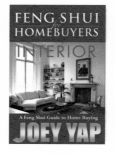

This book provides answers to the important questions of what really does matter when looking at the internal Feng Shui of a home or office. It teaches you how to analyze your home or office floor plans and how to improve the Feng Shui. It will answer all your questions about the positive and negative flow of Qi within your home and ways to utilize them to your maximum benefit.

Providing you with a guide to calculating your Life Gua and House Gua to fine-tune your Feng Shui within your property, Joey Yap focuses on practical, easily applicable ideas on what you can implement internally in a property.

Check Your Property's Feng Shui With Joey Yap's Mini Feng Shui Compass

Mini Feng Shui Compass

This Mini Feng Shui Compass with the accompanying Companion Booklet written by leading Feng Shui and Chinese Astrology Master Trainer Joey Yap is a must-have for any Feng Shui enthusiast.

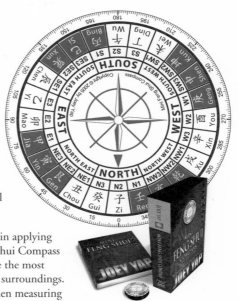

The Mini Feng Shui Compass is a self-aligning compass that is not only light at 100gms but also built sturdily to ensure it will be convenient to use anywhere. The rings on the Mini Feng Shui Compass are bi-lingual and incorporate the 24 Mountains rings that is used in your traditional Luo Pan.

A comprehensive booklet included will guide you in applying the 24 Mountain Directions on your Mini Feng Shui Compass effectively and the 8 Mansions Feng Shui to locate the most auspicious locations within your home, office and surroundings. You can also use the Mini Feng Shui Compass when measuring the direction of your property for the purpose of applying Flying Stars Feng Shui.

Accelerate Your Face Reading Skills With Joey Yap's Face Reading Revealed DVD Series

Face Reading Revealed – DVD 1
Introduction to Face Reading

Mian Xiang, the Chinese art of Face Reading is an ancient form of physiognomy and entails the use of the face and facial characteristics to evaluate key aspects of a person's life, luck and destiny. In this Introduction to Face Reading DVD, Joey Yap shows you how the eyes, ears, mouth, nose and eyebrows reveal a wealth of information about a person's luck, destiny and personality.

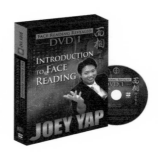

Face Reading Revealed – DVD 2
12 Palaces of the Face

Mian Xiang reveals not just a person's destiny and fortune, but talents, quirks and personality. Did you know that just by looking at a person's face, you can ascertain a wealth of information about their health, wealth, relationships and career? In this DVD, Joey Yap shows you how the 12 Palaces can be utilised to reveal a person's inner talents, personality quirks and much more.

Face Reading Revealed – DVD 3
100 Positions of the Face - Ages 1 to 30

Each facial feature on the face represents one year in a person's life. Joey Yap guides you through the 100 year map of the face and shares with you which features on your face govern your luck between the ages of 1 to 30. Also, learn how to deploy Fixed Position Face Reading and Multiple Position Face Reading techniques in this lively, entertaining and educational DVD.

Accelerate Your Face Reading Skills With Joey Yap's Face Reading Revealed DVD Series

Face Reading Revealed – DVD 4
100 Positions of the Face
- Ages 31 to 100

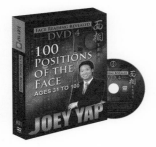

Your face is a 100 year map of your life but each position not only reveals your fortune and destiny for that age, but also reveals insights and information about your personality, skills, abilities and destiny. Delve deeper into the 100 year map of the face and discover, with Joey Yap, what facial features determine your luck between the ages of 31-100.

Face Reading Revealed – DVD 5
How to Read Face Shapes

This highly entertaining and insightful DVD shows you how just by evaluating the shape of a person's face, you can learn about their abilities, inclinations, personality and capacity in life. What does a Water face person excel in? What is the personality of a Metal faced person? Let Joey Yap show you the differences between the 10 character faces and how to discern the 5 basic element face shapes in this fun, entertaining and educational DVD.

Face Reading Revealed – DVD 6
The Significance of Moles, Hair and Birthmarks

Do moles have meanings? Yes, they do and in Face Reading, moles, birthmarks and even the type of hair on your head can reveal a lot about a person. Find out the meaning of moles on the face, what kinds of moles are favourable and unfavourable and whether or not you should remove certain moles with Feng Shui, Chinese Astrology and Face Reading Master Trainer Joey Yap.

Continue Your Journey with Joey Yap's Books

The Ten Thousand Year Calendar

The Ten Thousand Year Calendar or 萬年曆 Wan Nian Li is a regular reference book and an invaluable tool used by masters, practitioners and students of Feng Shui, BaZi (Four Pillars of Destiny), Chinese Zi Wei Dou Shu Astrology (Purple Star), Yi Jing (I-Ching) and Date Selection specialists.

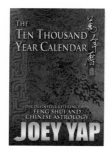

JOEY YAP's Ten Thousand Year Calendar provides the Gregorian (Western) dates converted into both the Chinese Solar and Lunar calendar in both the English and Chinese language.

It also includes a comprehensive set of key Feng Shui and Chinese Astrology charts and references, including Xuan Kong Nine Palace Flying Star Charts, Monthly and Daily Flying Stars, Water Dragon Formulas Reference Charts, Zi Wei Dou Shu (Purple Star) Astrology Reference Charts, BaZi (Four Pillars of Destiny) Heavenly Stems, Earthly Branches and all other related reference tables for Chinese Metaphysical Studies.

Stories and Lessons on Feng Shui

Stories and Lessons on Feng Shui is a compilation of essays and stories written by leading Feng Shui and Chinese Astrology trainer and consultant Joey Yap about Feng Shui and Chinese Astrology.

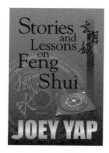

In this heart-warming collection of easy to read stories, find out why it's a myth that you should never have Water on the right hand side of your house, the truth behind the infamous 'love' and 'wealth' corners and that the sudden death of a pet fish is really NOT due to bad luck!

BaZi - The Destiny Code

Leading Chinese Astrology Master Trainer Joey Yap makes it easy to learn how to unlock your Destiny through your BaZi with this book. BaZi or Four Pillars of Destiny is an ancient Chinese science which enables individuals to understand their personality, hidden talents and abilities as well as their luck cycle, simply by examining the information contained within their birth data. The Destiny Code is the first book that shows readers how to plot and interpret their own Destiny Charts and lays the foundation for more in-depth BaZi studies. Written in a lively entertaining style, the Destiny Code makes BaZi accessible to the layperson. Within 10 chapters, understand and appreciate more about this astoundingly accurate ancient Chinese Metaphysical science.

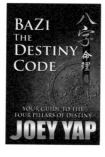

Continue Your Journey with Joey Yap's Books

Mian Xiang - Discover Face Reading

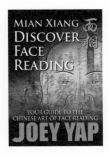

Need to identify a suitable business partner? How about understanding your staff or superiors better? Or even choosing a suitable spouse? These mind boggling questions can be answered in Joey Yap's introductory book to Face Reading titled 'Mian Xiang – Discover Face Reading'. This book will help you discover the hidden secrets in a person's face.

Mian Xiang – Discover Face Reading is comprehensive book on all areas of Face Reading, covering some of the most important facial features, including the forehead, mouth, ears and even the philtrum above your lips. This book will help you analyse not just your Destiny but help you achieve your full potential and achieve life fulfillment.

Xuan Kong - Flying Stars Feng Shui

Xuan Kong Flying Stars Feng Shui is an essential introductory book to the subject of Xuan Kong Fei Xing, a well-known and popular system of Feng Shui, written by the International Feng Shui Master Trainer Joey Yap.

In his down-to-earth, entertaining and easy to read style, Joey Yap takes you through the essential basics of Classical Feng Shui, and the key concepts of Xuan Kong Fei Xing (Flying Stars). Learn how to fly the stars, plot a Flying Star chart for your home or office and interpret the stars and star combinations. Find out how to utilise the favourable areas of your home or office for maximum benefit and learn 'tricks of the trade' and 'trade secrets' used by Feng Shui practitioners to enhance and maximise Qi in your home or office.

An essential integral introduction to the subject of Classical Feng Shui and the Flying Stars System of Feng Shui.

Feng Shui and Astrology for 2006

The Annual influences of each year play a crucial role in determining the Feng Shui of your property as well as your Destiny for the year 2006. Learn all about what 2006 holds in store for you with best selling author Joey Yap's new book - Feng Shui & Astrology for 2006.

This book will reveal the Feng Shui path ahead by charting out the Annual and Monthly Flying Stars, and explaining the influence the various sectors have on the occupants of the property. Based on your Chinese Zodiac animal sign, you will also be able to plan ahead using the Astrological guide for the year.

Discover the monthly guide to the Feng Shui of your home and learn how to manage it on a monthly basis as Joey Yap guides you with a clear explanation on what the effects will be and what you can do to mitigate them. Date selection is also a breeze with the auspicious dates for important activities already pre-selected in this book.

Elevate Your Feng Shui Skills With Joey Yap's Home Study Course And Educational DVDs

Xuan Kong Vol.1
An Advanced Feng Shui Home Study Course

Learn the Xuan Kong Flying Star Feng Shui system in just 20 lessons! Joey Yap's specialised notes and course work have been written to enable distance learning without compromising on the breadth or quality of the syllabus. Learn at your own pace and learn the same material students in a live class would learn. The most comprehensive distance learning course on Xuan Kong Flying Star Feng Shui in the market. Xuan Kong Flying Star Vol. 1 comes complete with a special binder for all your course notes.

Feng Shui for Period 8 - (DVD)

Don't miss the Feng Shui Event of the next 20 years! Catch Joey Yap LIVE and find out just what Period 8 is all about. This DVD boxed set zips you through the fundamentals of Feng Shui and the impact of this important change in the Feng Shui calendar. Joey's entertaining, conversational style walks you through the key changes that Period 8 will bring and how to tap into Wealth Qi and Good Feng Shui for the next 20 years.

Xuan Kong Flying Stars Beginners Workshop - (DVD)

Take a front row seat in Joey Yap's Xuan Kong Flying Stars workshop with this unique LIVE RECORDING of Joey Yap's Xuan Kong Flying Stars Feng Shui workshop, attended by over 500 people. This DVD program is an effective and quick introduction of Xuan Kong Feng Shui essentials for those who are just starting out in their study of classical Feng Shui. Learn to plot your own Flying Star chart in just 3 hours. Learn 'trade secret' methods, remedies and cures for Flying Stars Feng Shui. This boxed set contains 3 DVDs and 1 workbook with notes and charts for reference.

BaZi Four Pillars of Destiny Beginners Workshop - (DVD)

Ever wondered what Destiny has in store for you? Or curious to know how you can learn more about your personality and inner talents? BaZi or Four Pillars of Destiny is an ancient Chinese science that enables us to understand a person's hidden talent, inner potential, personality, health and wealth luck from just their birth data. This specially compiled DVD set of Joey Yap's BaZi Beginners Workshop provides a thorough and comprehensive introduction to BaZi. Learn how to read your own chart and understand your own luck cycle. This boxed set contains 3 DVDs, 1 workbook with notes and reference charts.

Interested in learning MORE about Feng Shui? Advance Your Feng Shui Knowledge with the Mastery Academy Courses.

Feng Shui Mastery Series™
™ LIVE COURSES (MODULES ONE TO FOUR)

Feng Shui Mastery – Module One
Beginners Course

Designed for students seeking an entry-level intensive program into the study of Feng Shui , Module One is an intensive foundation course that aims not only to provide you with an introduction to Feng Shui theories and formulas and equip you with the skills and judgments to begin practicing and conduct simple Feng Shui audits upon successful completion of the course. Learn all about Forms, Eight Mansions Feng Shui and Flying Star Feng Shui in just one day with a unique, structured learning program that makes learning Feng Shui quick and easy!

Feng Shui Mastery – Module Two
Practitioners Course

Building on the knowledge and foundation in classical Feng Shui theory garnered in M1, M2 provides a more advanced and in-depth understanding of Eight Mansions, Xuan Kong Flying Star and San He and introduces students to theories that are found only in the classical Chinese Feng Shui texts. This 3-Day Intensive course hones analytical and judgment skills, refines Luo Pan (Chinese Feng Shui compass) skills and reveals 'trade secret' remedies. Module Two covers advanced Forms Analysis, San He's Five Ghost Carry Treasure formula, Advanced Eight Mansions and Xuan Kong Flying Stars and equips you with the skills needed to undertake audits and consultations for residences and offices.

Feng Shui Mastery – Module Three
Advanced Practitioners Course

Module Three is designed for Professional Feng Shui Practitioners. Learn advanced topics in Feng Shui and take your skills to a cutting edge level. Be equipped with the knowledge, techniques and confidence to conduct large scale audits (like estate and resort planning). Learn how to apply different systems appropriately to remedy situations or cases deemed inauspicious by one system and reconcile conflicts in different systems of Feng Shui. Gain advanced knowledge of San He (Three Harmony) systems and San Yuan (Three Cycles) systems, advanced Luan Tou (Forms Feng Shui) and specialist Water Formulas.

Feng Shui Mastery – Module Four
Master Course

The graduating course of the Feng Shui Mastery (FSM) Series, this course takes the advanced practitioner to the Master level. Power packed M4 trains students to 'walk the mountains' and identify superior landform, superior grade structures and make qualitative evaluations of landform, structures, Water and Qi and covers advanced and exclusive topics of San He, San Yuan, Xuan Kong, Ba Zhai, Luan Tou (Advanced Forms and Water Formula) Feng Shui. Master Internal, External and Luan Tou (Landform) Feng Shui methodologies to apply Feng Shui at every level and undertake consultations of every scale and magnitude, from houses and apartments to housing estates, townships, shopping malls and commercial districts.

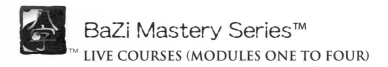

BaZi Mastery Series™
LIVE COURSES (MODULES ONE TO FOUR)

BaZi Mastery – Module One
Intensive Foundation Course

This Intensive One Day Foundation Course provides an introduction to the principles and fundamentals of BaZi (Four Pillars of Destiny) and Destiny Analysis methods such as Ten Gods, Useful God and Strength of Qi. Learn how to plot a BaZi chart and interpret your Destiny and your potential. Master BaZi and learn to capitalize on your strengths, minimize risks and downturns and take charge of your Destiny.

BaZi Mastery – Module Two
Practical BaZi Applications

BaZi Module Two teaches students advanced BaZi analysis techniques and specific analysis methods for relationship luck, health evaluation, wealth potential and career potential. Students will learn to identify BaZi chart structures, sophisticated methods for applying the Ten Gods, and how to read Auxiliary Stars. Students who have completed Module Two will be able to conduct professional BaZi readings.

BaZi Mastery – Module Three
Advanced Practitioners Program

Designed for the BaZi practitioner, learn how to read complex cases and unique events in BaZi charts and perform Big and Small assessments. Discover how to analyze personalities and evaluate talents precisely, as well as special formulas and classical methodologies for BaZi from classics such as Di Tian Sui and Qiong Tong Bao Jian.

BaZi Mastery – Module Four
Master Course in BaZi

The graduating course of the BaZi Mastery Series, this course takes the advanced practitioner to the Masters' level. BaZi M4 focuses on specialized techniques of BaZi reading, unique special structures and advance methods from ancient classical texts. This program includes techniques on date selection and ancient methodologies from the Qiong Tong Bao Jian and Yuan Hai Zi Ping classics.

XUAN KONG MASTERY SERIES™
LIVE COURSES (MODULES ONE TO THREE)
* Advanced Courses For Master Practitioners

Xuan Kong Mastery – Module One
Advanced Foundation Program

This course is for the experienced Feng Shui professionals who wish to expand their knowledge and skills in the Xuan Kong system of Feng Shui, covering important foundation methods and techniques from the Wu Chang and Guang Dong lineages of Xuan Kong Feng Shui.

Xuan Kong Mastery – Module Two A
Advanced Xuan Kong Methodologies

Designed for Feng Shui practitioners seeking to specialise in the Xuan Kong system, this program focuses on methods of application and Joey Yap's unique Life Palace and Shifting Palace Methods, as well as methods and techniques from the Wu Chang lineage.

Xuan Kong Mastery – Module Two B
Purple White

Explore in detail and in great depth the star combinations in Xuan Kong. Learn how each different combination reacts or responds in different palaces, under different environmental circumstances and to whom in the property. Learn methods, theories and techniques extracted from ancient classics such as Xuan Kong Mi Zhi, Xuan Kong Fu, Fei Xing Fu and Zi Bai Jue.

Xuan Kong Mastery – Module Three
Advanced Xuan Kong Da Gua

This intensive course focuses solely on the Xuan Kong Da Gua system covering the theories, techniques and methods of application of this unique 64-Hexagram based system of Xuan Kong including Xuan Kong Da Gua for landform analysis.

MIAN XIANG MASTERY SERIES™
LIVE COURSES (MODULES ONE AND TWO)

Mian Xiang Mastery – Module One
Basic Face Reading

A person's face is their fortune – learn more about the ancient Chinese art of Face Reading. In just one day, be equipped with techniques and skills to read a person's face and ascertain their character, luck, wealth and relationship luck.

Mian Xiang Mastery – Module Two
Practical Face Reading

Mian Xiang Module Two covers face reading techniques extracted from the ancient classics Shen Xiang Quan Pian and Shen Xiang Tie Guan Dau. Gain a greater depth and understanding of Mian Xiang and learn to recognize key structures and characteristics in a person's face.

Walking the Mountains! Learn Feng Shui in a Practical and Hands-on Program.

 Feng Shui Mastery Excursion Series™ : CHINA

Learn landform (Luan Tou) Feng Shui by walking the mountains and chasing the dragon's vein in China. This Program takes the students in a study tour to examine notable Feng Shui landmarks, mountains, hills, valleys, ancient palaces, famous mansions, houses and tombs in China. The Excursion is a 'practical' hands-on course where students are shown to perform readings using the formulas they've learnt and to recognize and read Feng Shui Landform (Luan Tou) formations.

Read about China Excursion here:
http://www.masteryacademy.com/Education/schoolfengshui/fengshuimasteryexcursion.asp

Mastery Academy courses are conducted around the world. Find out when will Joey Yap be in your area by visiting **www.masteryacademy.com** or call our office at +603-2284 8080 or +603-2284 8318.